FINAL
ACTS

FINAL ACTS

A Guide to Preserving the Records of Truth Commissions

TRUDY HUSKAMP PETERSON

Woodrow Wilson Center Press
Washington, D.C.

The Johns Hopkins University Press
Baltimore

EDITORIAL OFFICES
Woodrow Wilson Center Press
One Woodrow Wilson Plaza
1300 Pennsylvania Avenue, N.W.
Washington, D.C. 20004-3027
Telephone 202-691-4029
www.wilsoncenter.org

ORDER FORM
The Johns Hopkins University Press
Hampden Station
P.O. Box 50370
Baltimore, Maryland 21211
Telephone 1-800-537-5487
www.press.jhu.edu/books

Printed in the United States of America on acid-free paper
9 8 7 6 5 4 3 2 1

Library of Congress Cataloging-in-Publication Data

Peterson, Trudy Huskamp, 1945–
Final acts : a guide to preserving the records of truth commissions /
Trudy Huskamp Peterson.
p. cm.
ISBN 0-8018-8172-2 (pbk. : alk. paper)
1. Truth commissions—Records and correspondence—Conservation and restoration. I. Title.
JC580.P47 2005
025.1′96353462743—dc22
2004027087

Honorary Wilson Council Members

About the Center

The Center is the living memorial of the United States of America to the nation's twenty-eighth president, Woodrow Wilson. Congress established the

Woodrow Wilson Center in 1968 as an international institute for advanced study, "symbolizing and strengthening the fruitful relationship between the world of learning and the world of public affairs." The Center opened in 1970 under its own board of trustees.

In all its activities the Woodrow Wilson Center is a nonprofit, nonpartisan organization, supported financially by annual appropriations from the Congress, and by the contributions of foundations, corporations, and individuals. Conclusions or opinions expressed in Center publications and programs are those of the authors and speakers and do not necessarily reflect the views of the Center staff, fellows, trustees, advisory groups, or any individuals or organizations that provide financial support to the Center.

Contents

Preface

This study began with a phone call. Would I, asked Aryeh Neier, president of the Open Society Institute, go to South Africa and take a look at the records of the South Africa Truth and Reconciliation Commission? Of course I would. What I found at the commission, which was in the process of winding up its business, was a body of records of the greatest importance, unique in their contents and in the charged context in which they were created. Even more, the problem of future access to them would be extremely tricky, and the preservation of the records, both physically and intellectually, would be challenging. What institution could best manage this irreplaceable set of records? I recommended the National Archives of South Africa, and, after some stutter steps along the way, the records are now there.

During the years after that trip to South Africa, I watched as other truth commissions around the world—twenty have now completed their work—tried to grapple with the disposition of the records they had created. It became clear that, as different as the commissions were, they all had to ask themselves various legal, political, and archival questions when they finally had to decide what to do with their corpus of documents. Some commissions thought carefully about the records issues, but others appear not to have planned for preservation until the very end, and, as a result, records have been lost or misplaced.

This study began as an effort to provide current and future commissions with a set of questions to ask themselves, some commentary (but not answers—those must emerge from the individual context in which the commission operates) on those questions, and a description of the status of the records of commissions that have gone out of existence. The overview in Chapter 1 is designed for reading by commissioners and senior staff members. It is followed in Chapter 2 by a list of questions, grouped by legal, political, and archival issues. At times, the same general issue is considered twice, once as a legal matter and again as a political one. Chapter 3 contains a commentary on the list of questions, and Chapter 4 presents a set of country reports. Chapters 2–4 are more technical and may be of most interest to the archivists and administrative staff who are handling the records. Finally, the appendixes provide criteria for deciding distinguishing between records of a commission and the personal papers of commissioners and staff (Appendix A); considerations in determining access criteria (Appendix B); and physical storage standards for archival materials (Appendix C).

As I began tracing the records of the truth commissions covered in this study, I found that simply getting an answer to the question "Where are the records now?" was difficult in most cases and impossible in some. Although the primary purpose of the study is to assist the staff of active truth commissions, I hope that the country reports will also assist scholars by pointing them to the institutions that hold truth commission records and providing them with a capsule history of the journey of the records from their creation to their current custody.

The Woodrow Wilson International Center for Scholars funded this project, and I am immensely grateful to Lee Hamilton, Rosemary Lyon, and Christian Ostermann for supporting this proposal. The mistakes I have made are, of course, my own.

FINAL ACTS

CHAPTER 1

Overview

"All these things happened among us."

—*Mayan poem used as epigraph of the Report of the Truth Commission of El Salvador*

At the end of the tumultuous twentieth century, some countries seeking to learn what "happened among us" created a new institution, the truth commission. Although commissions vary from country to country, in general they are temporary bodies established to look at and report on a pattern of abuses by a repressive regime. They usually are established during or immediately after a transition from authoritarian to more democratic rule. About two dozen national truth commissions have been established over the past twenty years, most of them in the past decade and the greatest number in South and Central America, with Africa close behind.

When truth commissions open for business, they must focus on producing a report within the time allotted. To that end, a truth commission creates and receives a large quantity of information in a short period of time, often in less than two years. The commission recognizes that it must manage the flow of information of all kinds into its offices; however, until it nears the end of its existence, it rarely gives thought to what will happen to the records once it closes its doors. This guide is intended to assist commissions in the final disposition of their records. It is not intended to provide comprehensive guidelines for managing the records while in active use by the commission.

More specifically, this guide is directed at truth commissions created by a government or by an international body on behalf of a government to study a broad historical issue and report its findings directly to the country's chief executive or legislative body. These commissions create records that are government property (or, possibly, the property of intergovernmental organizations), and citizens have the right to demand preservation of and access to this government property. This study excludes truth commissions set up by nongovernmental bodies, important as they may be, because they and their records do not fall under the legal control of the government. Similarly, it excludes those commissions set up as a routine part of the government's business; the disposition of the records of these commissions is part of the routine disposition of the records of the government body to which they report.

Each commission is unique and so are the context in which it operates and the records it generates. Consequently, there is no single pattern for handling the records after a commission ceases to exist. Every commission should, however, consider certain questions when it decides what to do with its materials. This guide provides a list (Chapter 2) and then a discussion (Chapter 3) of those questions; a description of the practices of other commissions, so far as they are known (Chapter 4); and some best practices from archives around the world in deciding how to answer the questions (Chapter 3 and Appendixes).

WHY PRESERVE AT ALL?

Governments enact laws to govern property, and records are a type of property. The overriding question is why preserve the records at all? Why not let the report (assuming that there is a public final report) stand on its own? The records are often voluminous; they contain both substantiated and unsubstantiated allegations about living persons; establishing rules for access to the records will be difficult; and physically preserving some of them may be a problem. Why not just destroy them all?

For one thing, saving the records completes the commission's work. Oppressive regimes try to impose selective amnesia on society. The purpose of a truth commission is to break through that wall of silence and restore knowledge of the hitherto hidden hands in history. Destroying the records ensures that only those things that made their way into the report will be remembered officially, and thereby opens the way for persons opposed to the commission to win yet again. Saving the records ensures that amnesia does not prevail.

Another reason to save the commission's records is to demonstrate to future citizens how the commission operated, how it handled its charge, and what it did and did not know—in short, its legitimacy. The records document the operation of the commission with unparalleled immediacy and integrity.

Finally, information that the commission could not fit into its explanatory pattern may, with the eventual emergence of more information, finally make sense. Every generation asks new questions of historical evidence for two reasons. First, additional information becomes public, leading to a reevaluation of previous evidence. Second, new issues become public concerns, and the historical evidence is then reinterpreted in light of these new concerns. Future researchers will bring questions to the records beyond those the commission was required or able to ask under the terms of its charter and the state of its knowledge. The records will give those researchers the source materials to find answers to questions as yet unformed.

But just saving the records is not enough. They must be *preserved,* or the databases, audiotapes and videotapes, photographs, and even papers will deteriorate. All these items need attention if the information they hold is to survive. Records can speak across decades, providing evidence of the transactions of the commissions and information about the people, places, and phenomena that the commission investigated. But they must survive to speak, and that survival will depend on professional management of the records.

LAW AND COMMISSIONS

Records made or received during the conduct of government business belong to the government. Governments usually establish standard procedures for managing their records, both while in active use and when they are no longer needed for current transactions. Although commissions are a truly exceptional body of government, they arguably fall within the general administrative controls of the government, including the controls over the records the commission makes or receives. The international commissions established by an outside body such as the United Nations do not fall under government controls; they fall under the general controls of the United Nations, including the controls over records.

Other types of laws also may affect the ultimate disposition of the records of commissions. The first is a *national archives law,* which may or may not specify that the records of a commission must be turned over to the national archives at the conclusion of its work. The second law is a national *freedom of information act* or *habeas data act,* which defines the public's access to records of government bodies. Whether the commission is the type of body covered by such a law, if the country has one, must be determined. The third type of law is a *privacy act* or *data protection act,* which defines the personal privacy rights applicable to information held by the government. The applicability of a privacy act, like a freedom of information act, to the records of the commission must be determined. But whether a commission is covered by freedom of information or privacy acts or not, the disposition of the records must acknowledge the general principles the country has established through the acts. The fourth type of national law is an *open government* or *sunshine law,* which specifies what meetings of government must be open to the public. Again, even though this law may not apply to the commission, the general principle is that the records of an open meeting continue to be open, and that guideline should be followed in dealing with the records of the open meetings of the commission.

SCOPE OF THE RECORDS

The records of a commission include *all physical types* used in its work: paper, desktop electronic applications such as e-mail and word processing, databases, maps and drawings, still photographs, audiotapes, and videotapes. Although the records do not technically include associated physical objects, such as exhibits used in public hearings, the commission will often dispose of these objects together with its records.

The records of a commission are both those *created* by it and those *received* by it from other sources, including from other parts of government, from victims or their families, from nongovernmental organizations, or from the general public. If certain items have been provided to the commission under the condition that they will be returned to the lender, these issues must be resolved before the final disposition of the records. In general, these items should be copied before the original is returned. Similarly, if the records include items that have security classifications, the institution receiving the commission's records must have storage appropriate to hold records at that level of classification.

All working files are part of a commission's records. Commissioners and staff members should keep *personal papers* that do not relate to the conduct of commission activities separate from the commission's records. If this distinction has not been made before the commission closes, it should, at all costs, be made before staff members depart. Departing staff must not remove commission records, just as they would not remove any other government property.

Many commissions use *consultants* and *contractors* to carry out part of their work.[1] A commission must determine what parts of the materials generated by these vendors should be acquired and retained. This determination should be made before the commission shuts down, but the records from the vendors can be delivered either to the commission or to the institution receiving the commission's records.

ADMINISTRATIVE RECORDS, PROGRAM RECORDS, AND INVESTIGATIVE RECORDS

Commissions create three types of records: (1) administrative files, such as those on personnel, payroll, and fiscal matters; (2) program records, which document the substantive work of the commission; and (3) investigative records, which are related to particular individuals or incidents. Usually separate people or units within the commission handle these activities, and the records are therefore usually filed separately.

Administrative Records

Most administrative records pertain to the internal operation of the commission. In addition to personnel and financial records, these often include mailing lists of individuals and organizations, extra copies of reports and studies, and routine publications received from other government agencies or private organizations, such as copies of government regulations.

Administrative records can be destroyed in a relatively short period of time after the commission ceases to exist. Many governments have general records schedules that specify how long such records must be kept. Even though the time period is short, it will probably be longer than the life of the commission. The administrative records, identified as such, can be transferred to either the receiving institution for the program records or the part of government that provided administrative support for the commission during its existence. That successor custodian will retain the files until the expiration of the standard time period or until any audit or other legal action is completed.

Program Records

Program files include both the public and nonpublic management of the commission's activities, including the production of its report. Included in these records are:

- Meeting files: records of meetings held in executive session and generally consisting of the agenda, minutes or recordings of meetings, and briefing materials for members
- Public hearings files: edited and unedited transcripts and/or audiotapes and/or videotapes of the hearings
- Press conference files: edited and unedited transcripts and/or audiotapes and/or videotapes of the hearings
- News release files: one copy of each release issued by the commission
- Speech files: one copy of each speech by commissioners related to the mission of the commission
- Publication files: one copy of each published report, study, pamphlet, booklet, poster, photograph, audiotape or videotape, or other items produced by or for the commission. For the final report or major interim reports, drafts may be included
- Audiovisual files: still pictures, sound recordings, video recordings, and related documentation provided to the commission, such as news reports about the work of the commission

- Files of high officials: biographical materials about officials, correspondence and related records maintained by commissioners and key commission staff such as the chairman, executive director, legal counsel, or public relations officer
- General correspondence files: letters received and copies of letters sent about the work of the commission, including correspondence with other government agencies, other governments, private companies, organizations, institutions, and private individuals.

Program records document the workings of the commission. Items that explain the rationale leading to a commission's recommendations and conclusions are included in this category. Although some small amount of the records, such as routine correspondence with the general public, may be disposable, all of the program records should be preserved and transferred to a permanent successor custodian. That custodian may determine whether parts of the files can be destroyed with no loss to the historical record and will document any such disposal.

Investigative Records

Investigative records include files on individual cases or specific incidents, plus the databases and audiovisual materials that support the investigation. These records document the essential investigations, the purpose for which the commission was created. They also are the part of the commission's records that are most likely to be in demand as soon as the commission closes. All these records must be preserved and transferred to the successor custodian.

SELECTING A SUCCESSOR REPOSITORY

Persons responsible for selecting a successor repository must decide whether the records of the commission will be held by a government entity. If so, which one? If not, will they be held by a private organization in the country, or by an organization outside the country?

The keys to making these choices are the trust the public has in the integrity of the successor repository and the uses to which the records will be put. Particularly in governments where reforms are just beginning to take hold, the issue of trust is very difficult to resolve. As Rudolfo Mattarollo, the former deputy executive director of the United Nations Civilian Mission in Haiti, has written: "Safeguarding the evidence of the acts committed—one of the primary objectives of a truth commission—means safeguarding the circumstantial, documentary and material evidence, as well as testimony obtained from victims and witnesses."[2] Commissions must trust their successors to safeguard the records.

The only records that have been stored outside the commission's country are the records of the UN-sponsored truth commissions in Burundi, El Salvador, and Guatemala. Some commissions, including that of El Salvador, have considered placing their records with a custodian outside the government but inside the country, either an existing institution or one created specifically to handle the records of the commission. Although this may be the only solution if the entire government is deemed untrustworthy, international opinion, as the archivist of South Africa notes, "is swinging towards the view that sensitive records of repressive regimes should be kept by the national archives of the democratic successor states, not in special institutions."[3]

The other factor is subsequent use. If a commission's records are going to be used for future prosecutions, they must be placed in a repository where the prosecutors and defense counsels can have access. If the records of particular cases are to be available to the victims or their families, the repository must have facilities that make such access possible, and it should not be intimidating to these people who have already been traumatized by the actions of the state. If any part of the records is to be available for academic research, now or in the future, the records must be placed in a facility where finding aids can be produced and the records made available for research use.

Finally, a government must think about the costs of preserving the records and making them available. Nearly every government in the world supports its own national archives. It is less expensive to fund a single national archives than to operate two archival institutions, one the national archives and one the archives of a truth commission. In countries where little money is available for *any* archival institution (and that includes many of the countries where truth commissions operate), cost should be weighed when considering proposals to establish a new facility for the commission's records.

Whatever repository is ultimately chosen, the fundamental requirements are security for the records, clear access rules applied fairly, and a trustworthy custodian.

THE RIGHT TO KNOW

As the distinguished legal scholar Louis Joinet wrote in his influential report to the United Nations Commission on Human Rights on the question of impunity of perpetrators of human rights violations, the right to know

> is not simply the right of any individual victim or closely related persons to know what happened, a right to the truth. The right to know is also a collective right, drawing upon history to prevent violations from recurring in the future. Its corollary is a "duty to remember," which the State must assume, in order to guard against the perversions of history that go under the names of revisionism or negationism; the knowledge of the oppression it has lived through is part of a people's national heritage and as such must be preserved.[4]

Joinet proposed two series of measures to protect the right to know. One of the two was to preserve the "archives relating to human rights violations." Although Joinet focused on the government's records during the period of human rights violations, a logical extension of his argument is that the records of the commissions that investigated these violations must also be preserved and made available to succeeding generations. Adopting such an approach means establishing a framework for making the records available, while protecting the legitimate privacy and related rights of the people named in the records. Democracy is best served by a clear, consistent application of a publicly stated access policy. No matter what repository has the records, access rules are essential. Then, as the haunting line from the Mayan poem says, people will know that "all these things happened among us," both the violations and the attempt by a commission to uncover the truth.

NOTES

1. A contractor is a person or company that arranges to supply materials or workers. A consultant is a person who is a specialist in a particular subject and whose job is to give advice and information.
2. Rodolfo Mattarollo, "Truth Commissions," in *Post-Conflict Justice,* ed. M. Cherif Bassiouni (Ardsley, NY: Transnational Publishers, 2002), 299.
3. Graham Dominy, "A Delicate Balancing Act at the National Archives," *ThisDay* (South Africa), November 17, 2002.
4. "The Administration of Justice and the Human Rights of Detainees: Question of the Impunity of Perpetrators of Human Rights Violations (Civil and Political). Revised final report prepared by Mr. Joinet pursuant to Sub-Commission decision 1996/119," United Nations Commission on Human Rights, Sub-Commission on Prevention of Discrimination and Protection of Minorities, E/CN.4/Sub.2/1997/20/Rev.1, October 2, 1997.

CHAPTER 2

Questions to Consider

The disposition of the records of a truth commission is influenced by the legal context, the political context, and the archival context existing at the time the commission closes. The questions that any truth commission must ask itself in each of the three areas follow. Chapter 3 explores the issues that affect the answers to the questions.

LEGAL CONTEXT

LC.1. Does the legal instrument (law, order, resolution) that created the commission specify what institution should receive the records at the conclusion of the commission?

Applicability of Archives and Information Laws

LC.2. Does the country have an archival law? Does the archival law cover the records of the commission (i.e., is it a state body in terms of the records law)?

LC.3. Does the country have a freedom of information act? Does the act cover the records of the commission?

LC.4. Does the country have a privacy act or a data protection act? Does the act cover the records of the commission?

Applicability of Property Laws

LC.5. If the commission was created by order of the chief executive, do both the records of the commission and the final report belong to the president? Is the disposition of the records of the chief executive covered by law?

LC.6. If the commission was created by order of the legislature, do both the records of the commission and the final report belong to the legislature? Is the disposition of the records of the legislature covered by law?

LC.7. If the commission was created by order of an international body, do both the records of the commission and the final report belong to that body? Where are the records of that international body held?

LC.8. Do the rules governing the records of the government clarify what are the records of the government and what are personal papers? What controls exist over what documents a commissioner or staff member may remove? What are the controls over what documents contractors and consultants may remove?

LC.9. Is there a legal prohibition against removing from the country the records of the government? Does that prohibition cover the records of the commission?

Ownership of Submissions

LC.10. If original records or copies of records were submitted to the commission by government bodies, was the condition for submission that the documents would be returned to the submitters when the commission completed its work?

LC.11. If private organizations or individuals submitted documents to the commission, was the agreement that the items submitted be returned to the submitters when the commission completed its work?

Confidentiality and Access

LC.12. If the legal instrument establishing the commission states that the proceedings of the commission are to be confidential, what is the duration of that confidentiality? Is it a blanket closure, or is access permitted for certain purposes or for certain categories of individuals?

LC.13. If access is to be provided to some part of the records of the commission and if the legal instrument establishing the commission does not specify the criteria to be used in reviewing the records for disclosure, who will establish the review framework? On what principles?

POLITICAL CONTEXT

PC.1. Does the commission believe that the political change that occasioned the creation of the commission is irreversible? Do the citizens believe that the change is irreversible?

Reputation and Reliability of the Custodial Institution

PC.2. Has the institution where the commission is considering placing the records been implicated in past abuses? Has it been reformed? Have key staff members been changed?

PC.3. To what part of government does the institution under consideration by the commission for placement of the records report? How independent of the superior body is the institution?

PC.4. If access to some of the records is to be permitted to certain categories of researchers, such as the families of victims, are there institutions that, if holding the records, would have a reputation that would discourage the public to come for access to records?

Destruction

PC.5. Is it politically necessary to retain all the records? Is it politically necessary to destroy some or all of the records?

PC.6. Is there a real risk that the records will be disarranged, defaced, or destroyed in whole or in part if they are in the hands of operating (nonarchival) agencies?

Access

PC.7. Is access to the records necessary? For whom: prosecutors, subsequent commissions, government officials on official business, families of victims, academic researchers, journalists?

PC.8. Has the institution where the commission is considering placing the records had any experience in handling sensitive bodies of records? Where is the expertise for making access decisions?

Deposit Outside the Government

PC.9. Is it politically acceptable to deposit the records in a private or semiprivate institution within the country, such as a university or a foundation?

PC.10. If the records would not be safe—that is, protected from defacement or destruction—in the country, is it politically acceptable to deposit them outside the country? Is there an external institution that would be an acceptable home for them? Will the institution accept them? Can that institution provide access? Who will not be able to use the records if they are outside the country?

ARCHIVAL CONTEXT

Nature of the Records

AC.1. What physical types of records are included: papers, photographs, audiotapes and videotapes, databases, evidentiary objects?

AC.2. Are the administrative records (e.g., records dealing with personnel, payroll, fiscal matters) separate from the substantive records? If the commission's records fall under the national archives law, can these administrative records be destroyed after a fixed period of time? Is the work of the commission so exceptional that, for historical purposes, even the administrative records should be retained?

AC.3. If the commission had a Web site, will the archives or other institution holding the records be required to maintain the site online? For what period?

AC.4. If some of the work of the commission was public at the time it was created, such as public hearings or press releases, and if this public material will continue to be available to the public, is it clear which records are part of that publicly disclosable material?

Existing Capacity of Archives in the Country

AC.5. Does the national archives already hold the types of records that are part of the commission's records? Does another institution proposed as custodian of the records already hold these types of records?

AC.6. Does the national archives have experience preserving these types of records? Does another institution proposed as custodian of the records have experience preserving these types of records? What would it cost to provide such preservation?

AC.7. What level of security protection for records is provided by the national archives? Another institution? What would it cost to provide such protection?

AC.8. Does the national archives have research facilities for all the types of records? Does another institution? What would it cost to provide such facilities?

Personnel Qualifications

AC.9. What staffing is required to review the records of the commission for access? What are the qualifications for review staff? What training will be provided for review staff and by whom?

CHAPTER 3

Discussion of the Questions

The disposition of the records of a truth commission is influenced by the legal, political, and archival contexts in play at the time the commission closes. Each commission, when evaluating these contexts, may find the international models helpful, but even international best practices often prove impractical in the face of the actual situation in a country.

While the answers may vary from country to country, certain questions must be answered by each commission as it comes to a close. Ideally, these questions will be addressed at least six months before the commission's termination date to allow a seamless transfer of the records from the commission going out of existence to the institution that will take custody. Such a transfer is especially important if the act establishing the commission contains language such as "with the submission of its report the Commission will conclude its work and will automatically be dissolved." [1] Records that sit in empty offices are susceptible to pillage and destruction, and continuous official custody is the best guarantee that the records will survive intact.

LEGAL CONTEXT

LC.1. Does the legal instrument (law, order, resolution) that created the commission specify what institution should receive the records at the conclusion of the commission?

Most framers of enabling acts for truth commissions do not include the disposition of the commission records in the act. Perhaps unable to envision the situation at the conclusion of the commission's work, they are silent. Perhaps, too, framers assume that the final report is all the truth that should be revealed; yet a moment of reflection on the compromises made in any committee work and collegial writing project would lead to the conclusion that some information of significance is certain to be missing from the final report.

The act creating the truth commission in Peru specified that the records would go to the ombudsman's office when the commission finished its work.[2] By contrast, in Chile the act establishing the truth commission did not specify the disposition of the records, and so they were passed to its successor, the National Committee of Reparation and Reconciliation. When the latter expired in 1999, the government established the Human Rights Program in the Ministry of the Interior with the specific task of, among other things, keeping in "safe custody" the records of the committee.

Although inclusion of disposition language in the act should make the disposition easy, problems still may arise when the commission closes its doors. If, for example, the ombudsman's office is designated as the depository for the records but the ombudsman has neither the space nor the staff to handle the mass and variety of records created, a revision of the enabling act may be required. Or if the ministry of the interior is designated as the depository, but it becomes clear during the course of the investigation that the staff of the ministry has engaged in abuse of government power, the ministry may not be a politically comfortable custodian. In these cases, an amendment or revision may be required to change the designation.

Applicability of Archives and Records Laws

LC.2. Does the country have an archival law? Does the archival law cover the records of the commission (i.e., is it a state body in terms of the records law)?

Most countries now have an archival law.[3] How comprehensive it is (whether it covers all of the government or only part of it) and how modern it is (e.g., whether it covers electronic records) is a different matter altogether. Argentina, for example, has a national archives and an archival law, but a human rights activist stated flatly that the law is not an adequate "legal norm that regulates the functioning of national archives," and then she added, referring to the records of the Argentine truth commission, "much less this kind of archives."[4] Significantly, many archival laws do not cover the records of the legislature or the records of the chief executive, the two entities that have established the majority of the truth commissions. Furthermore, some countries exempt from the archives law those agencies whose records involve national security, including the ministries of interior.[5]

In Germany, the records of the commission established by the parliament were covered by the regulations on the records of the parliament,[6] and thus the commission records went to the parliamentary archives and from there to a foundation created by parliament. The Republic of Korea's Presidential Truth Commission on Suspicious Deaths is considered to be a public agency covered by the Public Records Management Act, and its records will go to the National Archives and Records Service of Korea.[7] In Peru, the commission was covered by the national archives law.[8] And in Zimbabwe, the records of the president's office for the period of the commission were transferred to the national archives for storage, presumably including the report (which was not made public) if not the records of the commission itself.[9] In other countries, such as Uruguay,[10] it is not clear whether the existing national archives law covers the records of the truth commission.

If the archives law covers the records but a specific instruction about the records in the legal instrument creating the commission differs from the archives law, how will the legal conflict be resolved? The commission in Peru found itself in this situation; an instruction in the commission's statute specified that the records were to go to the ombudsman's office, and the archives law specified that records of government bodies were to go to the national archives. Assuming that the commission instrument was passed after the archives law, it is reasonable to apply the principle that a second law is passed in full cognizance of the existence of the earlier law and that, if a provision conflicts, the second law prevails. If, in the case of Peru, the noncurrent records of the ombudsman's office will be transferred to the national archives, then there should be no hindrance to also transferring the truth commission records when the ombudsman's office has no further current use for them. If, however, the ombudsman's office does not fall under the provisions of the national archives act, then the ombudsman's office will be obliged to create its own archives.

LC.3. Does the country have a freedom of information act? Does the act cover the records of the commission?

The freedom of information movement has been most prominent in Western Europe, North America, and English-speaking lands. Six of the twenty countries with truth commissions covered by this study have freedom of information acts: Korea, Panama, Peru, the Philippines, South Africa, and Zimbabwe (ratification of the act is pending in Nigeria and Uganda). With the exception of the Philippines, which guaranteed freedom of information in its 1973 constitution, the other countries have all passed their laws since 1996. Korea's law was in place at the time the truth commission was created, and Panama, Peru, and South Africa all enacted the law during the period in which the commission was active. Zimbabwe passed its law in 2002, long after its truth commission was over, but the law is so restrictive that it has not provided an effective vehicle for access.[11]

South Africa's freedom of information act covers the records of the Truth and Reconciliation Commission (TRC) and has been used to obtain records. Korea's act also covers the its commission's records. The Commission on Human Rights in the Philippines, which inherited the records of the Philippine commission, is currently studying whether the law is applicable.[12]

Even if additional countries adopt freedom of information acts, their commission records may not be covered. Commissions most commonly report either to the country's chief executive or to its legislative body, and these two entities are often exempt from the working of a freedom of information act. Furthermore, an act may not be applicable retroactively and therefore might not cover records existing at the time the act was passed.

If a country has a freedom of information act and that act applies to the records of the commission, the custodian of the records will have to administer them in accordance with the act. This situation makes a good argument for retaining the records in a government archives that regularly handles records covered by the freedom of information act and not placing them in a nongovernmental institution. Although it would be possible to require an external organization to administer the records under the same access provisions required by a freedom of information act, working out such an arrangement would be complicated, particularly if the freedom of information act gives the requester the right to sue for access. Would government attorneys provide advice to the private institution during, for example, the processing of a request? Would government attorneys defend the private institution in the event of a lawsuit? How would the government ensure consistency in the application of the provisions of the law? It is less complicated to keep the records in government custody.

LC.4. Does the country have a privacy act or a data protection act? Does the act cover the records of the commission?

The constitutions of most countries include a right to privacy. Increasingly, countries are also enacting specific statutes protecting privacy, particularly since the advent of powerful computer systems that seem to threaten to breach personal privacy protections. In Europe, laws known as data protection acts are designed specifically to regulate the handling of personal data in computer systems. In 1981 both the Council of Europe and the Organisation for Economic Co-operation and Development (OECD) adopted specific rules for handling electronic data. Privacy International characterized these two agreements as having "a profound effect" on the handling of privacy data in countries around the world.[13]

Of the countries that have had truth commissions, Chile, Germany, and Korea have specific privacy or data protection acts, and Peru and South Africa are both drafting such laws. Germany's Federal Data Protection Law dates from 1977; Korea's was passed in 1994 and Chile's in 1999. Both Germany and Korea are members of OECD, which gives their handling of privacy information yet another layer of protection.

Germany's law does not apply to the truth commission records, because the records of a parliamentary commission fall under the special rules of the parliament. Korea's law appears to relate primarily to electronic data and so would not cover other types of commission records, such as paper or audiovisual items.[14]

As with freedom of information acts, even if additional countries adopt privacy or data protection acts, commission records may not be covered. Commissions most commonly report either to a country's chief executive or to the legislative body, and these two entities are often exempt from such an act. Furthermore, an act may not be applied retroactively, and therefore it might not cover records existing at the time the act was passed.

If a country has a privacy or data protection act and that act applies to the records of a commission, then the simplest course is to retain the records within a government archives that regularly handles records covered by the act and not place them in a nongovernmental institution. Even if a legal agreement could be framed to deposit materials covered by a privacy act outside the government, problems of consistency in administration of the act, legal advice, and defense in the event of a lawsuit are very difficult contingencies to address. It is easier to keep such records in a government institution.

Applicability of Property Laws

LC.5. If the commission was created by order of the chief executive, do both the records of the commission and the final report belong to the chief executive? Is the disposition of the records of the chief executive covered by law?

LC.6. If the commission was created by order of the legislature, do both the records of the commission and the final report belong to the legislature? Is the disposition of the records of the legislature covered by law?

Of the twenty countries with truth commissions covered by this study, three countries had commissions that were created by the parliament (Germany, Nepal, and South Africa), and fourteen had commissions that were created by and reported to the chief executive. (The other three were created by the United Nations—see question LC.7.) In either structure, the commission may obtain services from an executive agency, while maintaining its character as an independent government body. The South African Truth and Reconciliation Commission, for example, obtained administrative support services from the Ministry of Justice, even though the TRC was created by the parliament.

It is very difficult to determine whether the commissions established by and reporting to the chief executive are also part of the chief executive's office in terms of maintenance and disposition of records. Perhaps it is easier to answer that question in the reverse: if the records of the commission are not the chief executive's, are they part of the general records of the government? If a country had enacted a law on advisory committees, thereby bringing them into a regular relationship with government property laws (of which records laws are a subset), the records might be considered part of the general records of the government. That is the situation in Korea, where the National Archives and Records Service believes that the Public Records Management Act governs the records of presidential commissions, and that means the records go to the national archives.[15] Zimbabwe's 1985 Archives Act covers commissions "established by the Constitution" and corporate bodies established by act of parliament, but it is silent on commissions established by the president.[16] In the absence of a definitive statement, it is reasonable to assume that the records of a chief executive's commission fall under the control of the chief executive.

But what happens to the chief executive's records? Bolivia and Nigeria have archives laws that clearly cover the records of the president, and Chile and Peru have archives laws that do not exclude the presidential records. In Chile, however, the records of President Patricio Aylwin were sent to a nongovernmental organization, the Corporation Justice and Democracy (*Corporacion justicia y democracia*), which had been established under the president's guidance. Aylwin's records related to the National Truth and Reconciliation Commission, including the files of 3,877 cases of victims of human rights violations, were copied onto optical disks and the disks given to the national archives. The records of the commission itself were sent to the operating agencies rather than maintained with the records of the president.[17] The archives laws of Argentina and Zimbabwe appear to cover only the records of the ministries and other organs of state but not the presidency. As noted earlier, the Peruvian government had made specific provision in the commission language for the disposition of the records, so the fact that the president's records may be covered by the archives law was not a deciding factor in their disposition.

As for the commissions that reported to legislatures, the German commission's reporting relationship was unambiguous. The enabling act specified that the commission shall make "recommendation for action to the Bundestag with respect to legislative measures and other political initiatives"; that the commission's records were covered by the rules of the records of the parliament; and that the records were transferred to the archives of the parliament.[18] South Africa's commission was established by the parliament, but with powers that made it virtually an independent entity. It presented its final report to the president, but in truth presented it to the public. In creating the commission, the parliament did not specify the disposition of its records. As for Nepal, the Royal Nepalese Embassy in Washington, D.C., reported that the cabinet secretariat "would get the records," but the secretariat has not confirmed this.[19]

LC.7. If the commission was created by order of an international body, do both the records of the commission and the final report belong to that body? Where are the records of that international body held?

Three commissions—in Burundi, El Salvador, and Guatemala—were created with the assistance of the United Nations.

For Burundi, the UN Security Council asked UN Secretary-General Boutros Boutros-Ghali to establish an International Commission of Inquiry. The commission reported to the Secretary-General, who sent the commission's report to the Security Council. The logic is that the records of this commission would be the property of the UN Secretariat, and they were turned over to the Secretary-General, according to the commission's report. The records of the commission are now in the United Nations Archives and Records Management Section.[20]

The El Salvador Commission on the Truth was established as part of the Mexico Agreements of April 27, 1991, that ended the civil war in El Salvador. Under the provisions of the agreements, the truth commission was to consist of "three individuals appointed by the Secretary-General of the United Nations after consultation with the Parties." These provisions did not establish the ownership of the records the commission generated. The commission worked in El Salvador for approximately six months, then transferred its entire operation to the United Nations in New York. At the conclusion of the work, the records were transferred to the UN Archives in New York, where they are closed to research use for an indefinite period. In its report, the commission hoped that the records would be transferred to the law school of the U.S. university where a member of the commission was a law professor, but opposition in El Salvador scuttled this proposal.[21]

Emerging in circumstances similar to those of El Salvador's commission, Guatemala's Commission for Historical Clarification (CEH) was established pursuant to the Oslo Agreement of June 23, 1994, that ended the civil war in Guatemala. The head of the truth commission (the "moderator") was a foreigner, appointed by UN Secretary-General Kofi Annan. The moderator, in turn, appointed the two other members of the commission, who were Guatemalan. The United Nations Office for Project Services (UNOPS) provided the administrative and budgetary support for the commission; however, according to the moderator, "the United Nations took the view that the CEH, based on an agreement between the Government of Guatemala and the guerrilla organization, was not a UN institution even though the Secretary-General had agreed to appoint the coordinator and to publish the final report." The report was made to the government of Guatemala, the former guerrilla organization, and the UN Secretary-General.[22]

After issuance of the report, all records with "sensitivity" were shipped to the United Nations in New York, while nonsensitive records remained with the UNOPS in Guatemala. Any records that the "Coordinator of the Commission [the moderator] specifically designated in writing . . . as being for the public domain" were open; all the other records were physically sealed into containers to remain sealed until January 1, 2050, "or until such date thereafter as the Secretary-General may specify." As for unsealing the records, the Secretary-General "shall have regard" to the provisions of the Oslo Agreement, in particular the provision stating that "[t]he Commission's proceedings shall be confidential so as to guarantee the secrecy of the sources and the safety of witnesses and informants." The UN Archives, which has custody of the sealed records, interprets this provision to prohibit any access whatsoever, including access for the purposes of archival preservation.[23]

LC.8. Do the rules governing the records of the government clarify what are the records of the government and what are personal papers? What controls exist over what documents a commissioner or staff member may remove? What are the controls over what documents contractors and consultants may remove?

Every government must define the records it considers its official property. Usually this definition is part of the records or archives act, and is supplemented by regulations or guidelines issued by the national archives. Items that do not fall under the guidelines are usually considered personal property that can be removed when the person controlling the property leaves the office.

Because of the sensitivity of the records of truth commissions, it is particularly important that staff members and commissioners fully understand the difference between official records and personal property. That understanding should include an awareness of which original documents (including e-mail, databases, and audiovisual items) may be removed and of when a commissioner or staff member may make a copy of an item and remove the copy. As commissions draw to a close, staff members should be reminded of the distinction between records and personal papers, as defined by the government. If government regulations or guidelines are available, they should be given to staff members and commissioners. (If such guidelines are not available, they could consult Appendix A of this volume, which lists the questions to ask when determining whether documents are records or not.) Commissions should also consider instituting a checkout process whereby all persons leaving the commission are required to give written assurance that they have not removed any commission records.

Commissions often use contractors and consultants for specialized tasks, from exhumation to database management. Because consultants and contractors may use their own facilities, such as laboratories and computer systems, to perform the tasks assigned to them, information accumulates in these external sites. The contract with these outside parties should specify what happens to any documents given to and created by the parties, because then the ultimate disposition (e.g., transfer to the commission or destroy) of the consultant- or contractor-generated records is clear. If the contract does not specify the disposition, the commission will have to decide whether it wishes to negotiate an amendment to the contract to cover the disposition of such materials or whether it will trust in the discretion of that party.

LC.9. Is there a legal prohibition against removing from the country the records of the government? Does that prohibition cover the records of the commission?

All countries recognize the principle that public archives, by their nature and from the moment of their creation, form part of the movable public property of the state concerned and, as such, are subject to the property laws of the state. Public archives are deemed inalienable—that is, the sovereignty of a state prevents their removal or abandonment or transfer of ownership contrary to law.[24] If public records are removed from the state contrary to law, a successor state can initiate an action in replevin to obtain the return of the records.

This principle of inalienability applies to the records of a government truth commission. It means that a state would be required to take specific legal action, probably through legislation, in order to deposit the commission's records with a body outside the state, such as the United Nations. If the political climate in the country is volatile, the commission might recommend depositing the records outside for the country for at least a period of time. The commission may, however, find it difficult to obtain the legal authority to transfer the records, whether because of legislative lethargy, government resistance, or political considerations (for additional political considerations, see question PC.10).

An alternative is the external deposit of copies of commission records. Peru, for example, inquired whether the United Nations would act as a depository for a copy of the records of its commission, but the United Nations declined.[25] Some commissions have deposited copies of their databases with the American Academy for the Advancement of Science, which has provided various commissions with scientific and technical assistance.[26] Although the external deposit of the original records of the commission requires specific legislative action, the deposit of a copy of some part of the records may be an entirely administrative action and may be a sensible security precaution.

Ownership of Submissions

LC.10. If original records or copies of records were submitted to the commission by government bodies, was the condition for submission that the documents would be returned to the submitters when the commission completed its work?

Most commissions have complained about the lack of cooperation that they had from other government bodies during their investigations. The moderator of the Guatemala commission spoke for many, writing:

> [T]he armed forces pursued a deliberate strategy of obstruction without admitting this. Originally, the military mainly contended that the CEH had no right to see their archives, because most of the information was classified as secret. When the CEH protested this one-sided interpretation of its legal position, criticizing it as an attempt to frustrate the fulfillment of its mandate, the armed forces changed their strategy. They confined themselves to contending that the archives consisted of a black hole for the period under investigation by the CEH.[27]

A person who worked with Bolivia's commission, which was closed by the government before a report could be issued, commented: "We did not get records from the military or the secret police. We were not looking at all circumstances. We would send them written questions and we would get answers from the military. Mostly it would be answers that they had no information in the files."[28]

Some commissions, however, are given access to or copies of records held by the government—principally the government of the country in which the commission operates, but also occasionally the governments of other countries. Thomas Buergenthal has written tellingly of his attempts to get U.S. government documents for use by the commission in El Salvador; the Truth and Reconciliation Commission in South Africa had access to documents from both neighboring and European countries.[29] The majority of the problems, however, are with documents from national bodies.

Most commissions do not have the power to subpoena documents. The one commission that had the power, the TRC of South Africa, used it rarely. The TRC did get documents from both military and police files, but both groups wanted the commission to return both the originals and any copies made by the TRC. The originals were returned.[30]

A commission may sign an agreement with the originating body to establish how the records will be handled by the commission. If originals are provided, they will probably be a loan so that the commission's staff can make copies. Far more often, however, commissions get copies rather than originals, and probably copies with deletions. If the documents in question are classified, another level of complication arises. When South Africa's TRC had access to classified documents, it was not permitted to make copies but could ask for declassification. Most commissions only get declassified documents.

Whether the records are given to the commission by the originating body or loaned to the commission, they form part of the base of evidence used by the commission to make its judgments. Withdrawal of those critical documents from the files at the end of the commission will distort the subsequent evaluation of the commission's work. The possibility that the documents will be disclosed to future users often makes the creating agency anxious, and here the written agreement between the commission and the agency supplying the documents can be crucial. Classified documents, with national security markings, can be declassified only in accordance with the procedures of the government, which normally means that only the agency putting on the classification can remove it. Classified documents found in a body of commission records by a responsible custodian will be handled according to the existing regulations, and the mere fact of classification does not require the return of the classified records when the commission ceases to exist. Commissions should make every effort to retain this evidence.

LC.11. If private organizations or individuals submitted documents to the commission, was the agreement that the items be returned to the submitters when the commission completed its work?

A crucial part of any commission's work is obtaining evidence from nongovernmental sources. Often these sources are personal letters and photographs, or they may be records of or documents collected by organizations such as churches or nongovernmental organizations (NGOs). Sometimes, the items submitted by individuals are precious originals. Other submitters may provide copies, including copies of databases.

Like many commissions, South Africa's commission received documents from individuals. Some of these persons asked that their documents be returned to them, and some even asked that no copy be retained by the commission. Documents were apparently returned to these individuals.[31] Human rights activists in Zimbabwe provided that commission with reports and interviews with victims.[32] In Guatemala, three private databases—one from forensic anthropologists, one from a coalition of human rights groups, and one from the archdiocese of Guatemala—were made available to the commission for its use.[33]

A particular problem is the records acquired from guerrilla groups and opposition parties. The commission in El Salvador had difficulty obtaining information from the Farabundo Marti National Liberation Front (*Frente Farabundo Martí para la Liberación Nacional,* FMLN).[34] In South Africa, the African National Congress (ANC) was "slow" to turn over information, and the Inkatha Freedom Party was even more recalcitrant.[35]

The issue here is similar to that of the records of the government agencies: what is the agreement with the person or organization providing the document? And the problem is the same: how do you protect the body of evidence that the commission used to make its judgments if pieces of that evidence are given back to their owners without leaving a copy behind in the files? Once again, an obligation imposed on the commission by the owner of the materials becomes an obligation for the subsequent custodian of the commission's records, and any privacy protections continue in force. Every effort should be made to retain copies of these private documents.

Confidentiality and Access

LC.12. If the legal instrument establishing the commission states that the proceedings of the commission are to be confidential, what is the duration of that confidentiality? Is it a blanket closure, or is access permitted for certain purposes or for certain categories of individuals?

The mandates of some commissions include a statement that information given to the commission will be confidential. El Salvador's provision says that the commission's "activities shall be conducted on a confidential basis." Guatemala's provision says, "The activities of the Commission shall be confidential in order to guarantee the secrecy of the sources and the security of the witnesses and informants." Chile's decree says both that "[t]he Commission's activities will be confidential" and that "[e]ither on its own initiative or upon request, the Commission may take measures to protect the identity of those who provide information or assist in its tasks." Germany's law is conspicuously silent on the need for confidentiality, perhaps because the drafters recognized that the records would ultimately fall under the access laws protecting privacy in German records. Likewise, the mandates in Uganda and Chad are silent on the issues of confidentiality.[36]

The commission records of El Salvador and Guatemala, as noted earlier, are in the custody of the United Nations. According to the commission's chair, El Salvador's records are closed indefinitely, and Guatemala's are closed until 2050, unless authorized by the UN Secretary General "to protect the witnesses."[37] Chile reports that, although the commission's work is completed, "because trials are open, these archives are open for the moment only to lawyers and the Courts."[38]

If the purpose of a commission is to provide information to the public, then the confidentiality protection is not absolute. The issue is what categories of records must be closed and for what duration. Clearly, all records already made public or records of public events, such as open hearings, should remain open. Some commissions, upon closure, turn their records over to other government bodies for action. The Chilean commission is one example; in Haiti the records have been used by lawyers for the government.[39]

If the records of the commission are not open at some point to public scrutiny, then the only truth purveyed will be that in the final report. As many commissions know, the information in that report is a compromise, both among members of the commission and between the commission and political powers. As Reuters noted when the final report of South Africa's Truth and Reconciliation Commission was finally released in 2003, the report

> was delayed for almost a year because of a legal challenge by Zulu leader Mangosuthu Buthelezi to remove allegations of rights abuses by his Inkatha Freedom Party. The commission said its core findings remained intact, but it published a statement by Buthelezi denying the allegations. The commission has faced many legal challenges, including a last-minute suit by former president R. W. de Klerk, who forced the commission to black out some of its findings in its 1998 interim report. The bulk of those findings were printed in yesterday's report.[40]

Persons with interests in the records range from the victims and their families, to the alleged perpetrators, to the NGOs and other organizations that gave information to the commission, to journalists and scholars (see Appendix B for a discussion of considerations in determining access criteria). The fundamental principle must be that all records of the commission will, at some time in the future, be open for public inspection and research use. If they will never be open—not in a hundred years, not in a millennium—why preserve them? The issue is when, not whether.

LC.13. If access is to be provided to some part of the records of the commission and if the legal instrument establishing the commission does not specify the criteria to be used in reviewing the records for disclosure, who will establish the review framework? On what principles?

Attorneys, either from a ministry of justice, an ombudsman's office, or a human rights commission, most often establish the review criteria. An alternative is to establish an interagency body or a body that includes representatives of key external groups such as family organizations and ask that body to develop criteria.

Establishing the criteria does not mean conducting the review itself, although often the criteria are tentatively established by the body and then tested by a review of sample documents. Alternatively, the body can establish the criteria and leave open the option that it can reconvene to decide in instances in which the reviewers have difficulty applying the criteria to particular documents or document types.

At present, no international standard exists for access to records. UNESCO (the United Nations Educational, Scientific, and Cultural Organization) funded a study of the management of state security archives of repressive regimes that provides some guidance, although the records of state security archives are indeed distinct from the records of truth commissions.[41] In addition, the Council of Europe has adopted a European policy on access to archives, and the principles endorsed by the council can be tested against the records of the commission.[42] (Also see Appendix B for a set of access principles to consider when developing access criteria.)

POLITICAL CONTEXT

PC.1. Does the commission believe that the political change that occasioned the creation of the commission is irreversible? Do the citizens believe that the change is irreversible?

Although the usual declaration by supporters of a commission is "Never again!" the reality is that some commissions operate in a political environment that is more secure than others. In South Africa, for example, the commission worked in a tense political atmosphere, to be sure, but no one believed that apartheid would return. In Korea, too, the return of martial law is not a persistent fear. And Germany was certain the East German state would not rise again.

In El Salvador and Guatemala, by contrast, the commissions operated just after the peace accords, at a time of great instability. In Chile, Augusto Pinochet was still powerful, if not in power, when the commission concluded its work. The politics at the time of the commission's report in countries such as Bolivia, Haiti, Panama, and Zimbabwe can only be described as troubled.

Does the political environment make a difference? The evidence suggests that if the political change is perceived as final, the commission actively considers future public access to its records. The Truth and Reconciliation Commission in South Africa began examining the disposition and access questions before the commission issued its interim report.[43] The report of South Korea's commission included specific language on the disposition of its records and access to them.[44] Germany's commission from the outset had a plan for access to its records under the access provisions of parliament, as noted earlier. In the countries with more unstable political climates, access is often difficult or impossible. The records of the commissions in El Salvador and Guatemala are not in the country and are entirely closed. The commission records in Chile have had a complicated history (see the country report in Chapter 4), and they are not open for public use until prosecutors have completed their work. The records in Panama and Haiti are unavailable for public access, and even the physical location of the records is in question in Bolivia and Zimbabwe.

Reputation and Reliability of the Custodial Institution

PC.2. Has the institution where the commission is considering placing the records been implicated in past abuses? Has it been reformed? Have key staff members been changed?

A key political issue is trust: does the public trust the custodians of the records? Transparency International annually releases a Corruption Perceptions Index that measures the "perceptions of well-informed people with regard to the extent of corruption, defined as the misuse of public power for private benefit."[45] Seventeen of the twenty countries whose truth commissions are the subject of this study were ranked in the 2003 index—the index spans from 1 (the least corrupt country) to 102 (the most corrupt country). Only six of the seventeen ranked in the top fifty: Chile (17), Germany (18), Uruguay (32), South Africa (36), Korea (40), and Peru (45). Clearly, for most countries where commissions work, the level of public trust is low, even after the initial changes in government have been made.

Archives are, by their very nature, political, for they hold the records of regime and party. During dictatorships, they are particularly subservient to the dominant political power, because the records of regime and party are prime pieces of evidence about the nature and activities of the ruling elite.

Not all archives are equal participants during a dictatorship, however. Many countries have a divided archival system, with separate archives for the chief executive, the legislature, the courts, the ruling party, and the ministries of interior, defense, and foreign affairs, to name the most common divisions. In these systems, the national archives may have been immune to the most serious pressures to distort the historical record, because it held only the archives of less sensitive agencies and historical records with little current probative value. The national archives of Bolivia, for example, is reported to be a historical archives only.[46]

Nevertheless, problems in national archives have been documented. In Peru, for example, where the national archives reports to the Ministry of Justice, the records related to the citizenship status of President Alberto Fujimori were defaced while in the custody of the national archives, apparently to hide information detrimental to the president. Other related records may have been removed or destroyed.[47] The Uruguayan national archives, which reports to the Ministry of Culture, has also been questioned. In a public session at the 2003 annual meeting of the International Round Table of the Council on Archives, Alicia Casas de Barran of Uruguay commented: "Some people in national archives have been involved in dictatorial regimes and are still there." She wondered whether records would be well protected in such institutions, concluding that the placement of the records would depend on "individual circumstances in this regard."[48]

Two alternatives to depositing commission records in the national archives are to deposit them in the archives of the ministry of the interior or the ministry of justice. The problem of past practices and present reform is even more significant when considering these places of deposit. The archives within the ministry of the interior, which usually is also the ministry of the police, are part of an institution that was often part of the pattern of abuse. The archives within the ministry of justice may suffer from the same past affiliation. The relationship between the archives and its parent body then becomes the question.

PC.3. To what part of government does the institution under consideration by the commission for placement of the records report? How independent of the superior body is the institution?

The issue here is the politics of placement, and the fear is that even a trustworthy custodian may be subjected to irresistible pressures by an administratively superior body.[49] National archives have traditionally reported to one of three bodies: (1) the central organs of the state (i.e., the president or other head of state, the prime minister, the cabinet or council of ministers, or the secretary-general); (2) the ministry of education or culture or its equivalent; or (3) the home or interior ministry, including the ministry of justice. According to a 1993 worldwide survey by the International Council on Archives (ICA), in developing countries 29 percent of the national archives reported to the central authority, 48 percent reported to education/culture, and 15 percent reported to the ministries of interior/justice. Although only nine of the twenty countries with truth commissions participated in the ICA survey, the pattern of placement is the same.[50]

In only two countries are truth commission records known to be in or destined for the national archives: South Africa, where the national archives reports to the Ministry of Arts, Culture, Science and Technology, and Korea, where the archives reports to the Ministry of Government and Home Affairs (Interior).[51]

Three countries have deposited truth commission records with bodies reporting directly to the central authority. In Nepal, the records of the commission apparently went to the cabinet secretariat.[52] In Peru, the records went to the ombudsman's office, which is an independent (autonomous) institution within government.[53] In the Philippines, the records of the Presidential Committee on Human Rights went to the independent Commission on Human Rights.[54]

Most of the twenty countries have placed their commission records with the ministries of justice or interior. In Argentina, the records of the commission were deposited, by executive order, with the Secretary of Human Rights of the Nation in the Ministry of Justice, Security, and Human Rights of the Nation. This body is an integral part of the ministry, and the records "have played a central role in the administrative process necessary to achieve economic reparations of victims." [55] In Chad[56] and in Haiti,[57] the records went to the Ministry of Justice. In Bolivia, the commission was chaired by the minister of the interior, and because the commission closed before completing its work, it is assumed that the records were retained by the chair. The Ministry of the Interior in Bolivia has its own archives, and the presumption is that the records are there.[58] In

Chile, the records are in the Human Rights Program of the Ministry of the Interior.[59]

A look at the placement of another body of extremely sensitive records may be instructive. At the time of the reunification of Germany, the archival responsibility for the records of the Ministry for State Security (*Ministerium für Staatsicherheit* or "Stasi") of the former German Democratic Republic (GDR) was placed in a newly created government office called the Federal Commissioner for the Records of the Ministry for State Security of the Former GDR (familiarly known as the Gauck Authority). Many other countries have cited the creation of the Gauck Authority as a model for creating a separate body to handle sensitive records. Most of these recommendations for establishing a separate body to hold the records of truth commissions or other sensitive records stem from a misunderstanding of the German political situation at the time of reunification. The creation of the authority was a compromise between the two German governments, and, according to German archivists, one of the deciding factors in creating a separate entity was that the archives of the Federal Republic of Germany (FRG) were part of the Ministry of the Interior. Putting the Stasi records under the control of that ministry, and the fear that the ministry would impose severe restrictions on access or would even destroy part of the records, led to the creation of the separate body. While in no way denigrating the work of the Gauck Authority, German archivists now publicly regret the need to create this dual archives. According to Klaus Oldenhage, a senior German archivist, "The 'normal' public archival institutions can document human rights and the violations thereof for any past much better than any 'special' institutions, because public archives always have to guarantee a retrospective control of governments irrespective of their nature. Not just any archival institution should do this job, but the public archival institution." [60]

As the German example reveals, no subordinate body is truly independent of the superior body. The historical pattern, however, suggests that the least independent archives are within interior ministries. Archives reporting to the central state authority and those reporting to cultural ministries tend to have more latitude for independent judgments. A recent development is the placement of records with an ombudsman's office or with a human rights office, which, even if organizationally within justice or interior ministries, are usually very independent. The problems that develop in handling records in these offices tend to be archival in nature, not problems that result from a lack of independence (see the section "Archival Context" later in this chapter).

As Transparency International said in its "Global Corruption Report 2003," which examined access to information,

> Given that the systems the chief archivist manages and the records he or she holds provide the paper trails crucial for exposing mismanagement and corruption, we must question why these posts are so junior and under-resourced. Let us ask why the post of chief archivist is not accorded constitutional protection, and why it is not placed on a part with a supreme court judge or a supreme audit institution, so vital is its role in guaranteeing both accountability and public access.[61]

Any placement can work, but one that provides some degree of protection for the independent judgment of the professional managing the records is surely the most desirable.

PC.4. If access to some of the records is to be permitted to certain categories of researchers, such as the families of victims, are there institutions that, if holding the records, would have a reputation that would discourage the public to come for access to records?

Here there are two problems: the institution itself and the building it occupies. Victims will naturally be reluctant to visit a police department, a secret police headquarters, a justice ministry, or a military office to see their records. Explaining to a staff member of these groups what the person wants to see and then reading it under the watchful eye of a staff member would be daunting for most people, let alone someone who has been victimized by that institution. Putting the records in the custody of a more neutral institution is surely a better practice.

The building is a second issue. Fortunately, the records of truth commissions are small enough in size that the commission has a choice of buildings that can accommodate the records.[62] Countries have made a variety of choices: in current government buildings (the Philippines), in national archives (South Africa), or in rental space (Peru). All these choices must provide a visitor entry, security, an area in which the user can explain to a staff member what records he or she wants to see, and a research space.

Government buildings are often built to impress, to reinforce the power of the state. For many people, entering a government building is a daunting experience, and if it is the building of an agency that has harmed the person or the person's family in the past, the reluctance to enter may be great. Keeping the records in a government building may, however, be a reasonable choice if the records are being used by a successor agency for further investigation or prosecution. In such instances, the agency will have to make special efforts to provide a welcoming atmosphere for the users. National archives are usually in imposing buildings, but they are also established to provide user services. The national archives of South Africa, for example, is in a building that is designed with a friendly low façade, its name in multiple national languages engraved around the door, and easily accessible research areas. Rental space can be configured to make a research area that is sensitive to the needs of the users.

The most psychologically complex choice is to place the records in a building that is a symbol of past brutality. Argentina decided to turn a navy base that was a major torture center known as "Argentina's Auschwitz" into a museum to commemorate the people killed under the dictatorship. A human rights organization, Memoria Abierta, is collecting archival material for placement in the museum; it is not clear whether the records of the Argentine truth commission itself will be placed there.[63] Whether people will feel comfortable coming to do research in a place so freighted with a history of abuses is unknown.

One alternative that commissions and archives are adopting is to place some of the records and indices online for persons to use without having to encounter a staff member or enter a formal building. This solution, however, serves only those persons or their designees who have access to computer technology—a minority of the population in most countries where commissions have worked. In addition, sensitive case files and related records cannot be made publicly available online. The Internet is a useful tool, but it does not solve the access problems of the records of the truth commissions.

In choosing where to locate the records, commissions must consider both the institutional custodian and its reputation and the physical structure in which the records will be made available to the public. Balancing the needs of security and use by the government against the invisible barriers to research is important in order to serve all future users.

Destruction

PC.5. Is it politically necessary to retain all the records? Is it politically necessary to destroy some or all of the records?

Normal practice in government is to authorize the destruction of routine administrative and housekeeping records after their legal, fiscal, and administrative uses are fulfilled. In this category are financial records, personnel files, contracts, services agreements, and similar documents. As the archivist of Zimbabwe said, "If the records of the Commission include housekeeping records, they will be destroyed."[64] The problem is that the climate of suspicion between a government and its civil society may be so intense that even routine destruction is unwise. And in many if not most cases, it may be prudent for a government to announce publicly that it intends to destroy specified commission records and allow a period for public comment.

As for program and investigative records, some commissions have explicitly recommended preservation of some portions of these records. Korea's commission recommended prohibiting the destruction of records copied from government agency files and used by the commission: "The copied materials and records collected in the course of the investigations by the Commission, including the copied records of the government agencies such as the Government Archives, the national Intelligence Service, and the Military Intelligence Corps, should not be destroyed and be preserved in the records group of the Presidential Commission on Suspicious Deaths."[65]

Countervailing political pressures to destroy some or all of the program and investigative records may also exist. As noted earlier, South Africa's commission was pressured to return copies of classified records, and it was subject to pressures to expunge certain items from its report. Whether the latter pressures extended to destroying the underlying documents is not known. A Uruguayan activist, echoing the concerns of many in civil society, said that "there is concern that commission records turned over to the national archives "could be at risk of loss."[66] The commission records in El Salvador and Guatemala were moved outside the country to ensure their preservation. Asked if she agreed with that removal, Priscilla Hayner of the International Center for Transitional Justice and author of the definitive book on truth commissions, said swiftly, "Yes, I think the Guatemala and El Salvador materials should have gone outside the country for a time. The situation in the country was too dangerous to keep the materials there and safe."[67] The commission in Panama suffered a break-in after it completed its report, possibly by persons seeking to destroy records.

Although there have been some spectacular examples of governments destroying records to rid themselves of the past, such as the Greeks destroying sixteen million government files,[68] the more usual course is to retain the records but close them to public research use for a substantial period of time. If the only choice is between destruction and closure, closure is preferable.

PC.6. Is there a real risk that the records will be disarranged, defaced, or destroyed in whole or in part if they are in the hands of operating (nonarchival) agencies?

Disarrangement happened in Chile. In 2002 Chile began the process of nominating the Human Rights of Archives of Chile for inclusion in UNESCO's "Memory of the World" project.[69] The records of the Truth and Reconciliation Commission were not included, because, according to Chile's Memory of the World application, "once the Commission's mandate concluded, the documentation it had gathered and analyzed was transferred to other agencies, many of which have added or eliminated information." [70]

It is likely that all the commission records transferred for action by other bodies, such as the Argentine records used in the administrative process for economic reparations, have been disarranged. Similarly, it is likely that at least some disarrangement will take place when records are used for future prosecutions, such as the prosecution of the former president of Chad, or in human rights cases such as those in Haiti. Records may be removed from one file and incorporated into another; documents may be added to commission files; databases may be expanded. Such acts are typical during subsequent uses of commission records in many countries. Although future academic researchers may be unhappy that the pure commission record did not survive, the reality that the government must use the accumulated information takes priority. Archivists will keep the records as they were when last in active use—a principle known to archivists as the arrangement of "last current use."

Whether records have been defaced or destroyed is a different question. There are no known instances of defacement or destruction while records have been in the hands of operating successor agencies, but such information may not emerge until long after the acts occur. Furthermore, because the current location of the records of some commissions is not known, such as those of Bolivia and Uganda, it is possible that these records are in danger.[71]

Access

PC.7. Is access to the records necessary? For whom: prosecutors, subsequent commissions, government officials on official business, families of victims, academic researchers, journalists?

The relationship between the work of a commission and later or concurrent *prosecutions* is a vexing one. Some commissions erect a wall. In other countries, such as Chile and Haiti, the commission's records are used in prosecutions. The work of some commissions, such as those in the Philippines and in Chile, flows into *subsequent commissions* or government committees, which use the records.

Although *government officials on official business* are not normally denied access to a commission's records, that is precisely what has happened in El Salvador and Guatemala when those records were moved to the United Nations in New York and were closed to all users. In most countries, the records of a commission are available to the government for its purposes. But a distinction must be made between absorption of the records by another government body, which happened in the Philippines and in Chile, and access to the information in the records by officials. In the latter instance, the officials can read the records and (usually) obtain copies, but they may not withdraw the original record.

Of all outsiders, *victims and their families* are the most likely to be given access to the records about themselves. The report of Peru's commission was criticized by the victims, who had hoped that each case of persons missing and presumed dead would be accounted for in the commission's findings. As one Peruvian told the *New York Times,* the report of the commission was "all fine, but we want to know where they are."[72] According to a former staff member of the commission, the commission staff "always assumed that a sizeable portion of the documentation would be available to the public, to the relatives of victims and to researchers. That would mean an extract from the database would be made available. The question is what not to make available: the details, the information about perpetrators."[73]

Victims and their families typically have gained access to the file on their own case. Such access can be troublesome, however. For example, East Germans have the right to see the secret police file on themselves. Famously, some East Germans who gained access to their files learned that a spouse had informed on them and the marriage broke up; parents and children learned that they could not trust each other; neighbors were set against neighbors. Commissions are aware that the information they accumulate can identify both perpetrators and witnesses and could contribute to acts of revenge. In these cases, the "extract from the database" that Peru planned will have to be carefully programmed and the copy of the file will have to be redacted to eliminate certain information, under guidelines that are agreed on by the archives and by the lawyers who will defend the archives in the event of a legal action against it. Opening the file to the victims or the victim's family is not tantamount to opening the file to the public (Appendix B provides a set of access considerations in determining access criteria).

It is relatively easy to agree that victims have special rights of access to commission records; it is more complicated to provide *academic researchers and journalists* with access to those records. These researchers are not likely to confine their inquiries to one specific case, as the victims do, making the task of review to fulfill any specific request much more burdensome. Furthermore, assuming that access by one third party means that all subsequent third parties can have equivalent access, the review must proceed by assuming that anything that is released might be in the newspapers or posted on the Internet the next day.

Some commissions explicitly want the public to have access to the records of the commission. Korean recommendation 14-4 says, "The records should be utilized in extensive scale to find more facts and to be studied as historical sources," and recommendation 15-3 directs the government archives to "cooperate with other government agencies, civil societies, professionals, press, families of the victims, and the general public interested in the record to provide them with the convenience when they use the records."[74]

Several commissions also explicitly recommend obtaining records of previous regimes and, sometimes, making them available. Germany's commission, for example, was instructed to "strive primarily to achieve" the "obtaining, securing, and opening [of] the pertinent archives."[75] Korea's commission made some recommendations about the records of government, including the recommendation that records of intelligence and police agencies related to "state violence and human rights violations during the authoritarian regimes" be "preserved permanently and opened to the public for public interest."[76] The instruction to the commission in Chad was "to collect documentation, archives and exploit them," although not specifically to open them to the public.

PC.8. Has the institution where the commission is considering placing the records had any experience in handling sensitive bodies of records? Where is the expertise for making access decisions?

Other than exclusively historical archives, most archives (whether national archives or archives within a ministry) handle records that must be withheld from the public for a period of time. Some of the reasons to restrict access to records are privacy, national security, investigative information, or records designated by statute as closed.

The records of truth commissions have an extra degree of sensitivity, more akin to handling the records of secret police or public prosecutors than to handling regular government records. Furthermore, a distinction must be made between storing sensitive records and handling them. Many archives within ministries are simply controlled storage areas, where records are checked in and out for the parent organization. Those facilities are similar to a records center run by a national archives. As the archivist of Zimbabwe remarked, "We really don't know what we have [in the records center]. When records are sent from an office for records center storage we don't open the boxes and check each file. We just accept the transfer description and store them. The report [of the commission] should be in the records of the Office of the President and Cabinet for that period, but I really don't know."[77]

Handling records, including the processes of arranging and describing the records for use by secondary users (such as external parties), is much more complex and requires understanding both the records and the context in which they were created. Handling is also different from making access determinations either on classified records or on access to sensitive but unclassified records.

Archives almost never have the authority to declassify records. In a few national systems, a classifying authority—for example, the army—will give an archives specific instructions that a certain type of information is now declassified and that documents containing that type of information can be opened. In these cases, the classifying authority retains the right to review the work of the archives. Usually, however, the classifying authority comes to the archives and carries out the declassification with its own employees. If only a few documents are requested for declassification, the archives may duplicate the records and send the copies to the classifying office for review and decision. A more unusual alternative is to set up a panel to review the classified records. In South Africa, a multiagency team reviewed sensitive TRC records and formulated recommendations on what information could be released and what information required continued protection. Peru also established a review commission.[78] In the United States, a panel of external commissioners, created by a special act of Congress in 1992, reviewed and determined access on records related to the 1963 assassination of President John F. Kennedy.

In some countries, classification is applied only to national security and foreign policy information; in other countries, it is applied to any information that cannot be made freely available. In government systems with reasonably narrow classification schemes, a substantial body of records that are sensitive but unclassified exist and must be reviewed prior to release. Once again, two patterns seem to characterize this process. In some governments, the creating agencies may tell the archivists which records to open and which to hold closed, much like the process for classified records. In other governments, the archivists identify the records that must be closed, applying general criteria provided either by a freedom of information act or by general restrictions that the archives has developed for its holdings. In the United States, for example, the archivists at the National Archives and Records Administration (NARA) routinely review unclassified but sensitive records and make the final access determinations.

Because authoritarian regimes notoriously do not have public access policies, a country recently achieving democracy is unlikely to have any experience making access decisions. Among the countries that have had commissions, Germany had experience in making access determinations, because it was able to draw on the West German tradition. The value of working through the problem by using both archivists and legal advisers is considerable, because the decisions made will serve as a precedent for making decisions on other restricted records, such as the records of the secret police or of security bodies. In all repositories there will be a learning process, and it is useful to have that learning take place in an institution that will be able to rely on it for handling future accessions of government records.

Deposit outside the Government

PC.9. Is it politically acceptable to deposit the records in a private or semiprivate institution, such as a university or a foundation?

The Germans created a semipublic foundation to handle the records of the Commission of Inquiry on Working through the History and the Consequences of the SED Dictatorship. El Salvador's commission wanted to deposit its records with the university law school in Washington, D.C., where one of the commissioners taught, but objections in El Salvador eliminated that option. Guatemala's commission hoped that Guatemala's Congress would create a foundation with five principal mandates, one of which would be "promotion of and support for historical research." At least some of the commission records probably would have been deposited with such a foundation, but it was not created. A university in Uruguay has offered to hold the records of the Uruguayan commission.[79]

The problem with transferring the records to a private or semiprivate institution is twofold: first, because the records belong to the government, the government must be responsible for their preservation and maintenance; second, as records of a public function, they must be administered in accordance with the access rules of the public authorities. Satisfying these two conditions requires public control of the records. Although it is possible to assert public control over records in a private or semiprivate institution, such control creates an additional level of difficulty in handling these sensitive records.

But what if the government is unstable at the time the commission closes and general political opinion continues to see the government as untrustworthy? Does placing the records in a private institution help to keep them secure, or at least seem to be more secure? Certainly, such a step does not protect the records from search and seizure by government agents. Furthermore, there will over time surely be pressure to fund the archives out of the public purse, particularly if the costs of managing the archives are burdensome. This situation will raise the question of why pay for a separate archives when the national archives is already being funded by the government. Depositing the records in a private institution may be a temporary solution if the entire government or the national archives is deemed untrustworthy, but international opinion, as the archivist of South Africa notes, "is swinging towards the view that sensitive records of repressive regimes should be kept by the national archives of the successor democratic states, not in special institutions."[80]

PC.10. If the records would not be safe—that is, protected from defacement or destruction—in the country, is it politically acceptable to deposit them outside the country? Is there an external institution that would be an acceptable home for them? Will the institution accept them? Can that institution provide access? Who will not be able to use the records if they are outside the country?

As noted earlier (see question LC.13), some countries have laws requiring that records declared to be part of the fundamental records of the state, known as the "state archival fonds," cannot be taken outside the country. All of the European Union has adopted this practice, as have the countries that were once part of the Soviet Union. UNESCO has reinforced this practice by including it as part of the criteria for adding records to its Memory of the World list. Any country operating under such legislation is unlikely to be able to remove the records of a truth commission from the country.

Even if the records can be removed legally, it is not easy to find a suitable home. As noted earlier, the United Nations turned down Peru's request to hold a copy of its records. Large universities or manuscript repositories may be willing to house them, but only with the assurance of continued funding (and notice the failed attempt to place the El Salvadoran records at such an institution in the United States). If the plan is to deposit the records only until conditions in the home country improve (whereupon the records would be returned), the problems are compounded, because institutions do not wish to expend money on the preservation of records they know will not stay in their holdings. Further complicating the problems is the fact that most of the likely universities and manuscript repositories are located in nations that are former colonial powers or in nations that may have a historically tense relationship with the nation of the commission; governments may naturally be reluctant to place records in these countries.

Finally, the problems of defining access to the records multiply when the records are no longer in the country. Strict guidelines for making access determinations would have to be negotiated at the time of deposit, including who would do the screening. Access for victims and the families of victims would almost surely require the intervention of a third party, because victims are unlikely to be able to travel to the records.

ARCHIVAL CONTEXT

Nature of the Records

AC.1. What physical types of records are included: papers, photographs, audiotapes and videotapes, databases, evidentiary objects?

Truth commissions typically use the full range of physical types of records:

- *Paper* is currently the most common physical type. The paper records may include such varied materials as cartography, floor plans, and scientific reports of genetic mapping.
- *Databases* have been a feature of commission work since the early 1990s, and the use of *electronic systems* (both word processing and e-mail) is now common.
- *Photographs* may be submitted to the commission by the families of victims or by external organizations; they may also be photographs taken of the commission at work or of commission-sponsored activities such as exhumations.
- *X-rays and dental photographs* may be included in case files, if they were used for identification purposes.
- Commissions may make *audiotapes* of official interviews. The commission may also have copies of radio interviews given by the commissioners.
- Commissions may *videotape* their public hearings; they may also receive copies of television coverage of commission activities. In addition, some video may be taken of commission-sponsored activities.
- Commissions may receive *artifacts* from persons testifying or from exhumations, such as shreds of cloth or handcuffs. Although not technically records, these pieces of evidence are often held with the

records, and their disposition and preservation must be considered along with the case files to which they relate.[81]

The records of commissions are relatively voluminous. The German commission's records extend about 30 linear meters.[82] Peru's materials are estimated at 200 linear meters[83] and Argentina's at 130 linear meters.[84] These are quantities that require management planning.

Planning is also required to preserve and make available the wide variety of physical types found in the records. Bolivia's commission made audiotapes of sessions with witnesses, and the commission also received photographs from the families and reports from forensic doctors that may have included photographic materials.[85] In Burundi, the report says that "in the case of oral testimony" a tape recording was made and that "photographs or other exhibits" were transferred to the executive secretary of the commission.[86] The records of the commission in El Salvador, now held by the UN Archives, include electronic records, audiotapes, and videotapes.[87] The records of the German commission are entirely paper.[88] The records of Haiti's commission's included victim questionnaires, audiotapes of interviews, photographs in the reports of the forensic team, a database, documents given to the commission, and internal commission documents.[89] Korea's commission had videotapes and (probably) computer databases.[90] The commission in Peru had some objects.[91] The commission in the Philippines had paper and still photographs along with some physical objects.[92] South Africa's commission had every physical type: databases, still photographs, audiotapes and videotapes, and objects.

AC.2. Are the administrative records (e.g., records dealing with personnel, payroll, fiscal matters) separate from the substantive records? If the commission's records fall under the national archives law, can these administrative records be destroyed after a fixed period of time? Is the work of the commission so exceptional that, for historical purposes, even the administrative records should be retained?

Archivists typically judge administrative records to have no continuing historical value. These records are destroyed after their functional usefulness, including any audits of performance and expenditure, is completed. Many countries have "general records schedules," which specify the length of time that documents common to all government agencies—such as administrative records—are to be retained. The archivist of Zimbabwe, for example, pointed out that if the records of the commission included the administrative records, they would be destroyed in accordance with the general records schedules.[93]

Because the work of truth commissions is controversial, their administrative records may have to be retained for a longer period than required under the general schedules (if not retained permanently). Germany, for example, reports that its parliamentary archives will retain the commission's administrative records even after the rest of the records are transferred to the new foundation.[94] The Philippines, too, reports no destruction of administrative records.[95] The sealed records of El Salvador's commission include the administrative records.

Is this degree of caution warranted? Certainly for a time, the administration of the commission, its use of funds, its criteria for hiring staff and the qualifications of those hired, its security arrangements, and similar matters will remain important to the government, to the commission, and to its critics. If improprieties are alleged or proved, the records may have to be kept indefinitely. However, if the commission's administration is not challenged, in the long term the receipts for travel costs, the documents on rental of office space, and the applications for jobs have no lasting historical value and can be destroyed in accordance with general records schedules. One option may be to publish notice of the intent to destroy specified commission records and allow a period for public comment (see question PC.5).

AC.3. If the commission had a Web site, will the archives or other institution holding the records be required to maintain the site online? For what period?

A recent study found that most items live on Web sites for fifty-five months.[96] If the commission operates a Web site, it may wish to have the successor organization maintain the site, at least for a period of time, to facilitate access to information on the commission, particularly for journalists. The commission may wish to specify the length of time that the Web site must be maintained, leaving it to the successor whether to remove it at the expiration of that period. Or the commission may leave the decision entirely in the hands of the successor body.

The other question is whether the archives will be required to maintain a copy of the Web site as an archival item. Much recent debate has gone into the general question of maintaining Web sites. Assuming that everything that is posted on the Web site by the commission is a copy of a document found in the commission's records (i.e., that the items on the site are all duplicate copies), then the preservation of the Web site is a matter of simply saving the look and format of the site, giving future researchers an understanding of what was provided by the site and how. Various strategies are available for preserving this information. All of them, however, require the continuing migration of the site's information to new software (see question AC.6).

AC.4. If some of the work of the commission was public at the time it was created, such as public hearings or press releases, and if this public material will continue to be available to the public, is it clear which records are part of that publicly disclosable material?

While the commission is operating, certain records are public as soon as they are produced. These public records may include:

- Public hearings files, including transcripts and/or audiotapes or videotapes of the hearings
- Publications files, including one copy of each published report, study, pamphlet, booklet, poster, or other publication produced by or for the commission
- Press release files, including one copy of each release issued by the commission. Biographical backgrounds on each of the commissioners, with photographs, may be included.
- Speech files, including one copy of each speech by commissioners and senior staff members related to the work of the commission
- Press conference files, including the transcripts and/or audiotapes or videotapes of the press conferences held by the commission
- Clippings files, consisting of clippings about the commissioners and the commission, its work, its press releases and publications, and related materials.

It is often useful to maintain the commission's public records separately from other records, because all staff will know that the records in these series can be made available without further review. If the public records have been maintained separately, they can be made easily available after they are transferred to the subsequent custodian. If, however, the public records are mingled with nonpublic items (e.g., a transcript of a press conference is filed with the background briefing notes used by the person holding the press conference), the materials will have to be reviewed and the nonpublic records separated before external researchers can use the public records. It is essential that the succeeding custodian of the records understand whether there are purely public series or not.

Existing Capacity of Archives in the Country

AC.5. Does the national archives already hold the types of records that are part of the commission's records? Does another institution proposed as custodian of the records already hold these types of records?

National archivists traditionally have held paper. Today, most archivists recognize electronic media as an extension of paper and understand they must hold it, although they may not yet have had much experience with archival electronic records. Audiovisual materials, particularly audiotapes and videotapes, may or may not be part of the charge of the national archives. If they are not, then another institution in government—such as a national broadcasting company—holds these media for the government. Increasingly, however, electronic systems are merging word processing and data and audio and video files, either created digitally or copied into digital format. When these mixed electronic systems are transferred to an archives, the archivists will be responsible for the audio and video records, whether or not the government has a separate audio or video archives. Finally, any national archives holding court or police records will have had experience with associated artifacts.

Looking again at the countries where commissions have completed their work, the archives law in Argentina specifically excludes audiovisual records from the control of the national archives.[97] Bolivia's archival law does not eliminate any physical types, but the national archives reportedly holds only paper.[98] Chile's national archives law includes audiovisual materials; the archives laws in Ecuador, El Salvador, and Peru are general and could be read to include any physical type. The German and South African archival systems include the management of all physical types of records. The definitions of records in the archives laws of Korea, Nigeria, the Philippines, and Zimbabwe are very wide and include all physical types.[99]

For the non-national archives, the pattern is mixed. The UN Archives holds all physical types. The ombudsman's office in Peru probably has little experience with materials other than paper and, perhaps, simple office electronic systems. Ministries of justice have experience with objects and audiovisual items (e.g., still photographs, audiotapes of interrogations, videotapes from surveillance cameras) obtained as evidence, but probably little experience with maintaining electronic records. The German foundation established to handle the German records is a new institution and therefore has no prior holdings.

It is desirable that the custodian of the records of a commission have experience in handling all the physical types of materials that are in the commission's records. In particular, it is important that the archives either already has the knowledge and skills to handle electronic records or is able to obtain that support from another trusted source. As commissions rely increasingly on electronic systems, the ability to preserve electronic information becomes crucial for the ultimate custodian. Indeed, the need to handle electronic records is common to all national archives, because all governments now utilize, to some extent, electronic records. Placing the commission records in the national archives should reinforce or help to build the capacity to handle electronic records to the general benefit of the archival program for the entire government.

AC.6. Does the national archives have experience preserving these types of records? Does another institution proposed as custodian of the records have experience preserving these types of records? What would it cost to provide such preservation?

Even though a law empowers a national archives to hold various physical types of records, the archives may not have an active preservation program for those formats. Germany, Korea, and South Africa do have ongoing programs for the physical preservation of both paper and nonpaper materials in their archives.

Of the other institutions proposed as custodians, the UN Archives is working on the preservation of still photographs as well as its paper holdings. It is unlikely that government agencies in a country where a truth commission has operated—that is, other than the national archives or another cultural agency—would have experience in preserving either paper or nonpaper records.

Preservation costs include, at minimum, the physical housing of the materials, the staff to maintain the holdings, and the supplies for preservation. The costs vary by climate, by labor costs within the country, and by the availability or nonavailability of preservation supplies within the country. Housing costs are principally those of maintaining the proper temperature and humidity for the physical types of materials to be stored. A table with the recommended storage conditions appears in Appendix C.

Paper records must be housed in acid-free boxes and, if possible, in acid-free file folders. Large metal items that will rust, such as binder clips or prongs, should be removed. Records that are in binders or clamps should be removed and placed in file folders.

Electronic records include both the electronic records themselves and the documentation of the computer systems on which they were made and received. The documentation for commonly used desktop applications is quite simple to obtain and retain, but the documentation for custom-designed applications must be captured before the system is shut down by either the commission or the contractor. These include file specifications, user guides, output specifications, codebooks, input forms, record layouts, editing procedures, and reports.

The cost of preserving electronic records also includes the cost of recopying (migrating) the information every five years, or as often as the software or hardware on which the original records were recorded becomes obsolete. Until a stable electronic preservation medium is found (and none has been found to date), recopying will be an ongoing cost.

Audiovisual materials also have significant preservation costs. Audiotapes and videotapes must be duplicated and the copy used for research to ensure that the master is not accidentally damaged during use. Copies must be made of still photographs as well. If the only photograph is a print, which will be true in many cases, then a negative must be produced (and, ideally, a reference print as well), or the print will have to be scanned and only the scanned image provided for research use.

AC.7. What level of security protection for records is provided by the national archives? Another institution? What would it cost to provide such protection?

All commission records must be secure from tampering and pilferage. Within that secure storage, two specially protected areas may need to be established, one for records containing national security information and one for especially sensitive but unclassified records.

Commissions work in space that is at least generally secure—that is, it includes locks, guards, perhaps alarm systems, perhaps smoke detectors or sprinklers, as well as vaults or combination lock safes or filing cabinets with combination locks. The facility that receives the commission's records must have at least equivalent storage conditions.[100]

Most national archives operate secure storage areas protected by at least rudimentary locks. Some may have special areas for storage of more sensitive materials. Still others may have areas approved by the security agencies for storage of security-classified records. Some have round-the-clock guards; others have guards only during the day and rely on alarms during nights and weekends. If the archives is going to house the records of a commission, it may have to upgrade its security.

Facilities in ministries such as justice or interior may have space that is more secure against outside intrusions than the space available to the national archives. The problem with the records space in most ministries, however, is that it is not secure against unauthorized access by insiders. Consequently, placing the records of a commission in the ministry's space may require constructing internal barriers to minimize the possibility of tampering. In Haiti, for example, the records of the commission are reportedly stored in a "special room" at the Ministry of Justice.[101]

Rental space is also a problem, because typically it will not have adequate levels of security. Governments renting space for the storage of sensitive records will have to agree with the owner that adequate security can be installed, ranging from alarms to additional interior walls. In Peru, the ombudsman's office had neither the staff nor the space for the records, and so the government of Belgium provided money to lease space for six months,[102] a time period so short that physical security arrangements probably could not be completed before the lease expired.

AC.8. Does the national archives have research facilities for all the types of records? Does another institution? What would it cost to provide such facilities?

If the records are to be used and not simply stored, the institution housing them must also have facilities for public access. The public space must be separate from the records, which must be in locked areas that the public cannot enter by accident or design. The room used by the public must be equipped with the facilities needed for using records of all types, including computers for accessing databases and finding aids, players for listening to sound recordings, and stations for watching videotapes. Finally, it is important that the research rooms be monitored by staff at all times when records are in use to ensure that records are not disarranged or damaged or destroyed.

The situation in Peru is instructive. The ombudsman's office had no money for desks or staff or supplies, and the Belgian funds were for the lease only—that is, for space but not for research facilities.[103] Ministries are unlikely to have adequate public access facilities. Conversely, national archives routinely operate public research rooms with staff monitoring users.

Personnel Qualifications

AC.9. What staffing is required to review the records of the commission for access? What are the qualifications for review staff? What training will be provided for review staff and by whom?

At least four different types of review are required to make commission records available for public users. The first and simplest is the review to separate the records already made public from those that have not (see question AC.4). The second is the review of nonpublic records according to predetermined criteria so that those that do not meet the criteria for public release can be withdrawn. This kind of review is required for making records available to the general research public, including academics and journalists. The third is the review of records about a victim so that the person, the person's family, or the person's authorized agent can have access to the records. This review may require copying documents in order to delete parts of them before making them available. The fourth type of review is of items with security markings to determine whether they can now be declassified. Each of these types of review requires different levels of expertise and different lengths of time.

All staff that review records must be detail-oriented persons who understand general access rules and apply them to specific records. They must be employees who can be trusted not to transmit information obtained from restricted records except as required in the course of their official duties. Individuals handling security-classified information must be cleared by the appropriate government bodies. The review for public/nonpublic records can be done by general records staff under the guidance of professional archivists; this is usual work within an archives. Review under established criteria is more complex; a common practice is to have the initial review done by a general staff member and a second review handled by an archivist. If an advisory panel has been established (see PC.8 above), the archives may refer difficult decisions to it and also may ask it to review training materials developed by the archives. Professional staff members usually handle review for release to victims, consulting with the archives' lawyers as necessary; final copying and deletion can be done by general staff members and reviewed by archivists. The lawyers should provide training on the review of victim records. Persons with the requisite clearances must handle declassification, but again general staff members can complete the initial review with a second review by archivists.

If commission records are placed in the national archives, over time the national archives will build a body of precedent in the handling of this type of sensitive records. This precedent will enhance the capacity of the national archives to handle other sensitive bodies of government records. As each succeeding body of sensitive records is deposited, the staff's expertise expands and the government's and the public's confidence in the national archives grows. Both developments benefit the current and future governments.

NOTES

1. "Decree Establishing the National Commission on Truth and Reconciliation [in Chile], Supreme Decree no 355 (April 25, 1990), Article 4," in *Transitional Justice: How Emerging Democracies Reckon with Former Regimes,* 3 vols., ed. Neil J. Kritz (Washington, D.C.: United States Institute of Peace Press, 1995), 3:101–104.

2. Eduardo Gonzalez, former staff member, Peruvian Truth Commission, interview by author, New York City, November 19, 2003.
3. *Archivum,* Vol. 40, Archival Legislation 1981–1994, Albania–Kenya; Vol. 41, Archival Legislation 1981–1994, Latvia–Zimbabwe.
4. Valeria Barbuto, staff member, Memoria Abierta, e-mail message to author, October 6, 2003.
5. Bolivia, for example, exempts the Ministry of Interior from the requirement to transfer records to the national archives because of national security and authorizes it to maintain its historical records. *Archivum,* Vol. 40, Bolivia.
6. Matthias Buchholz, archivist, Stiftung zue Aufarbeitung der SED-Dikatur, e-mail messages to author, September 24, 29, 2003.
7. Sangmin Lee, chief consultant archivist, National Archives and Records Service, Republic of Korea, e-mail message to author, September 28, 2003.
8. Eduardo Gonzalez, interview by author, November 19, 2003.
9. Ivan Munhamo Murambiwa, national archivist of Zimbabwe, interview by author, Capetown, South Africa, October 23, 2003.
10. Alicia Casas de Barran, professor, Universidad de la Republica, Escuela Universitaria de Archivologia, Uruguay, interview by author, Capetown, South Africa, October 21, 2003.
11. Panama enacted its freedom of information act on January 22, 2002; Peru, August 2002 (it became effective January 2003); South Africa, February 2000 (it became effective March 2001). David Banisar, "The *freedominfo.org* Global Survey: Freedom of Information and Access to Government Records Laws around the World," September 28, 2003, http://www.freedominfo.org (accessed December 5, 2003).
12. Graham Dominy, national archivist of South Africa, e-mail message to author, December 8, 2003; Sangmin Lee, e-mail message to author, December 9, 2003; Jacqueline B. Veloria-Mejia, director, Commission on Human Rights, Philippines, e-mail message to author, December 2, 2003.
13. Privacy International is a human rights group formed in 1990 as a watchdog on surveillance and privacy invasions by governments and corporations. Based in London, it produces, with www.freedominfo.org, an annual global survey of freedom of information and access to government records around the world.
14. http://www.privacyinternational.org/survey/phr2003/countries (accessed December 5, 2003).
15. Sangmin Lee, e-mail message to author, September 28, 2003.
16. *Archivum,* Vol. 41, National Archives Act, 1985, Zimbabwe, 268–272.
17. Gloria Alberti, UNESCO regional officer, Chile, e-mail message to author, November 28, 2003.
18. "Law Creating the Commission of Inquiry on 'Working through the History and the Consequences of the SED Dictatorship,'" Act No. 12/2597, May 14, 1992, paragraph 4, in Kritz, *Transitional Justice,* 3:216–219.

19. Krishna Chandra Aryal, first secretary, Royal Embassy of Nepal, interview by author, Washington, D.C., September 29, 2003.
20. "Final Report, International Commission of Inquiry" and letter from the Secretary-General to the president of the Security Council, S/1996/682, July 25, 1996; Bridget Sisk, archivist of the United Nations, e-mail messages to author, October 17, 2003 and May 21, 2004.
21. Thomas Buergenthal, "The United Nations Truth Commission for El Salvador," *Vanderbilt Journal of Transnational Law* 27 (October 1994): 497; "El Salvador: Report of the Commission on Truth," in Kritz, *Transitional Justice,* 3:177–215; Bridget Sisk, interview by author, New York City, December 1, 2003; Monique Hand for Thomas Buergenthal, former commissioner, El Salvador Commission on the Truth, e-mail message to author, January 30, 2004.
22. Christian Tomuschat, "Clarification Commission in Guatemala," *Human Rights Quarterly* 23, no. 2 (2001): 233–258; "Guatemala: Agreement on the Establishment of the Commission for the Historical Clarification of Human Rights Violations and Incidents of Violence that Have Caused Suffering to the Guatemalan Population," in Kritz, *Transitional Justice,* 3:220–222; Secretary-General's Bulletin, Commission for Historical Clarification, ST/SGB/1999/6, June 8, 1999; Bridget Sisk, interview by author, December 1, 2003.
23. Secretary-General's Bulletin; Bridget Sisk, interview by author, December 1, 2003; Christian Tomuschat, moderator, Commission for Historical Clarification, e-mail message to author, February 4, 2004.
24. Peter Walne, ed., *Dictionary of Archival Terminology.,* 2d ed. (Munich: K. G. Saur for the International Council on Archives, 1988).
25. Eduardo Gonzalez, interview by author, November 19, 2003.
26. Audrey Chapman, director, Science and Human Rights Program, American Association for the Advancement of Science, interview by author, Washington, D.C., February 9, 2004.
27. Christian Tomuschat, "Clarification Commission in Guatemala," *Human Rights Quarterly* 23, no. 2 (2001): 250.
28. Confidential communication, September 25, 2003.
29. Buergenthal, "United Nations Truth Commission for El Salvador"; Graham Dominy, e-mail message to author, December 8, 2003.
30. Priscilla Hayner, *Unspeakable Truths: Confronting State Terror and Atrocity* (New York: Routledge, 2002), 42; Trudy Huskamp Peterson, "Report: Records of the Truth and Reconciliation Commission," June 25, 1998.
31. Peterson, "Report."
32. Michael Auret, former chair, Catholic Commission for Justice and Peace, Zimbabwe, e-mail message to author, February 9, 2004.
33. Audrey R. Chapman and Patrick Ball, "The Lesson of Truth Commissions: Comparative Lessons from Haiti, South Africa, and Guatemala," *Human Rights Quarterly* 23, no. 1 (2001): 1–43.

34. Buergenthal, "United Nations Truth Commission for El Salvador."
35. Hayner, *Unspeakable Truths,* 42.
36. Kritz, *Transitional Justice,* Vol. 3.
37. Christian Tomuschat, e-mail message to author, February 4, 2004.
38. Gloria Alberti, e-mail message to author, December 9, 2003.
39. Brian Concannon, attorney, Bureau of International Lawyers, e-mail message to author, September 24, 2003.
40. "South Africa's Tutu Urges Apartheid Reparations" (Reuters), *Boston Globe,* March 22, 2003, http://www.boston.com/dailyglobe2/081/nation/S_Africa_s_Tutu_urges_apartheid_reparations+.shtml (accessed March 22, 2003).
41. Antonio Gonzalez Quintana, "Archives of the Security Services of Former Repressive Regimes: Report Prepared for UNESCO," UNESCO, Paris, 1997.
42. "Recommendations (2002)2 on Access to Official Documents, 21/02/02, Meeting 784"; "Recommendations (2000)13 on a European Policy on Access to Archives, 13/07/00."
43. Peterson, "Report."
44. "Report of the Presidential Commission on Suspicious Deaths; the First Report, 2000.10 to 2002.10," Presidential Commission on Suspicious Deaths, Seoul, January 2003, recommendations 14 and 15, p. 282; translation by Sangmin Lee, copy in author's possession.
45. Transparency International is an international nongovernmental organization based in Berlin and devoted to combating corruption at both the national and international levels.
46. Confidential communication, October 3, 2003.
47. Confidential communication with official of Ministry of Justice, October 2, 2003; Eduardo Gonzalez, interview by author, November 19, 2003.
48. Alicia Casas de Barran comments, October 22, 2003; notes in author's possession.
49. Fear that the superior body, the General Services Administration (GSA), would require the U.S. National Archives and Records Service to destroy the famous audiotapes of President Richard Nixon led to the removal of the National Archives from the GSA and its reassignment to report directly to the president.
50. Michael Roper, "The Present State of Archival Development World-Wide." Paper presented to the Inter-Regional Conference on Archival Development, Tunis, May 16–20, 1995. Copy in author's possession.
51. Act of Management of Records of Public Agencies, Government of Korea; copy in author's possession.
52. Krishna Chandra Aryal, interview by author, September 29, 2003.
53. Javier Ciurlizza, former executive secretary, Truth and Reconciliation Commission of Peru, e-mail message to author, October 7, 2003.
54. Jacqueline B. Veloria-Meija, e-mail message to author, December 1, 2003.
55. Valeria Barbuto, e-mail message to author, October 6, 2003.

56. Abdoulaye Beri, first counselor, Embassy of Chad, Washington, D.C., interview by author, September 25, 2003. The commission in Chad investigated the crimes of former president Hissene Habre; it was not a general truth commission. With the current Belgian indictment of Habre, the records may be in use.
57. Brian Concannon, e-mail message to author, September 24, 2003. The archivist of Haiti, Jean-Wilfrid Bertrand, suggested that the records might have been divided between the Ministry of Justice and the Ministry of the Interior, but the government has not confirmed that. Jean-Wilfrid Bertrand, interview by author, Capetown, South Africa, October 22, 2003.
58. *Archivum,* Vol. 40, Bolivia, 71–76.
59. It appears that the records of the National Truth and Reconciliation Commission passed to the National Committee of Reparation and Reconciliation, which was the official successor. The committee expired in 1999, and the Human Rights Program of the Ministry of the Interior was entrusted with the task of keeping and leaving "in safe custody the documents and files of the former National Committee of Reparation and Reconciliation."
60. Klaus Oldenhage, speech at the International Round Table of the Council on Archives, Capetown, South Africa, October 2003; copy in author's possession.
61. Jeremy Pope, "Access to Information: Whose Right and Whose Information?" in *Global Corruption Report 2003,* Transparency International, http://www.globalcorruptionreport.org/download/gcr2003/03_Access_to_information_(Pope).pdf, p. 21.
62. This is in sharp contrast to the records of secret police, for example, where the tens of thousands of linear meters of records often preclude moving them to another facility. The Gauck Authority that took over the records of the East German secret police, for example, had little choice but to administer the records in the buildings where they were housed: in this case, the custodian of the records changed, but the building did not.
63. "Argentina to Turn Its 'Auschwitz' into Rights Museum," New York Times Online News Report, February 10, 2004, http://wwww.nytimes.com; "Debate Rises in Argentina on Museum of Abuses," *New York Times,* April 19, 2004, A13.
64. Ivan Munhamo Murambiwa, interview by author, October 23, 2003.
65. "Report of the Presidential Commission on Suspicious Deaths," recommendation 15-2.
66. Confidential communication.
67. Priscilla Hayner, interview by author, New York City, November 19, 2003.
68. "Symbolic Healing of Greek Civil War's Wounds," *New York Times,* August 30, 1989, with a spectacular photograph of the archives ablaze. See also Quintana, "Archives of the Security Services," section 3.1, for discussion of the Greek decision and the opposite decision by Spain to preserve the police archives of the Franco regime. See Chapter 4, "Chile," for further discussion.
69. In 1992 UNESCO launched the "Memory of the World" Programme to facilitate preservation by the most appropriate techniques of the world's documentary

heritage, to assist access to it without discrimination against any users, and to increase the awareness worldwide of its existence and significance. Nations nominate documentary holdings to a Memory of the World Register.

70. UNESCO application in possession of Gloria Alberti; reviewed by author on October 22, 2003.
71. Records of the Uganda Commission of Inquiry, which operated from 1986 to 1995, are not in the custody of the Ministry of Public Service, which controls records storage for the government. The assistant commissioner wrote: "My guess is the Office of the President would still be in custody of the full report." Robert Okusam, e-mail message to author, November 18, 2003.
72. The report found that 69,280 people died during twenty years of brutal conflict in Peru. Most victims were Quechua-speaking Indians; half of those estimated to have died were not identified by the commission. "Truth Commission Leaves Many in Indians in Peru Unsatisfied," *New York Times,* August 31, 2003, A10.
73. Eduardo Gonzalez, interview by author, November 19, 2003.
74. "Report of the Presidential Commission on Suspicious Deaths," recommendations 14–4 and 15–3.
75. "Germany: Law Creating the Commission of Inquiry on 'Working through the History and the Consequences of the SED Dictatorship,'" in Kritz, *Transitional Justice,* 3:216–219.
76. "Report of the Presidential Commission on Suspicious Deaths," recommendation 2, especially 2–2.
77. Ivan Munhamo Murambiwa, interview by author, October 23, 2003.
78. Graham Dominy, "A Delicate Balancing Act at the National Archives," *ThisDay* (South Africa), November 17, 2002; Eduardo Gonzalez, e-mail message to author, Mary 17, 2004, forwarding the ombudsman's resolution creating the review commission.
79. "From Madness to Hope: The 12-Year War in El Salvador," Report of the Commission on the Truth for El Salvador, United Nations Publication, S/25500, 1993; excerpt in Kritz, *Transitional Justice,* 3:177–215; Thomas Buergenthal, e-mail message to author, January 30, 2004; "Commission for Historical Clarification Report," English translation of summary and recommendations, http://hrdata.aaas.org/ceh; Alicia Casas de Barran, interview by author, October 21, 2003.
80. Dominy, "Delicate Balancing Act."
81. Human remains found as part of the commission's work are not part of the commission records, but they are a by-product of commission activities. In Peru, for example, the exhumations were carried out under the authority of the prosecutor general, and once the remains were identified, they were given to the family.
82. Matthias Buchholz, e-mail message to author, September 24, 2003.
83. Eduardo Gonzalez, interview by author, November 19, 2003.
84. Laura Saldivia, lawyer, Secretary of Human Rights, Ministry of Justice, Argentina, e-mail message to author, February 9, 2004.

85. Confidential communication, September 25, 2003.
86. United Nations Security Council, S/1996/682, August 22, 1996, Appendix I.
87. Bridget Sisk, e-mail message to author, February 17, 2004.
88. Matthias Buchholz, e-mail message to author, September 24, 2003.
89. Brian Concannon, e-mail message to author, September 24, 2003.
90. "Report of the Presidential Commission on Suspicious Deaths," recommendation 15-1: "The Government Archives should classify and preserve the records of the Commission (all related textual records and video tapes)."
91. Eduardo Gonzalez, interview by author, November 19, 2003.
92. Jacqueline B. Veloria-Mejia, e-mail message to author, December 2, 2003.
93. Ivan Munhamo Murambiwa, interview by author, October 23, 2003.
94. Matthias Buchholz, e-mail message to author, September 24, 2003.
95. Jacqueline B. Veloria-Mejia, e-mail message to author, December 2, 2003.
96. "ONLINE," *Chronicle of Higher Education,* May 3, 2002, A31, reporting on study by John Makewell and David W. Brooks in *Journal of Science Education and Technology* (June 2002).
97. *Archivum,* Vol. 40, Argentina.
98. Confidential communication, October 3, 2003.
99. *Archivum,* Vols. 40 and 41.
100. Even taking these precautions, some commissions have found their records in danger. The office of the commission in Panama, for example, was burglarized several times, as noted earlier. *Panama News* (biweekly), June 22–July 5, July 6–19, and August 17–September 6, 2003, http://www.ThePanamaNews.com (accessed February 17, 2004).
101. Brian Concannon, e-mail message to author, September 24, 2003.
102. Eduardo Gonzalez, interview by author, November 19, 2003.
103. Ibid.

CHAPTER 4

Country Reports

During late 2003 and early 2004, I studied twenty government truth commissions to determine what happened to their records. I limited my survey to commissions that (1) were established by the government as a whole (by the chief of state or by the legislature), (2) considered broad historical events, and (3) had completed their work. I had several reasons for these limits. First, although some truth commissions established by non-governmental organizations have played important roles in precipitating regime change, their records are private, not public, property. By contrast, the truth commissions established by governments create records that are government property, and citizens have the right to demand preservation of and access to these records. Second, I wanted to avoid looking at investigating commissions at lower levels of government, such as the commission created by the Ministry of Government and Police in Ecuador, because their records should simply fall within the records controls for that body. The commissions that present problems in the disposition of records are those that exist at the top of a government, particularly those that include public sector participation or participation from various parts of the government. Third, I wanted to know what had happened, not what might happen, to commissions, so I excluded the active commissions (e.g., those in Ghana, Sierra Leone, and East Timor). The twenty commissions I studied are all the commissions that met my three criteria.

My study was supported by the Woodrow Wilson International Center for Scholars in Washington, D.C. Using the center's resources, I sent the following questions in either English or Spanish to the national archives in each of the twenty countries:

- What kinds of records did the commission create?
- Where are the records now?
- Are they divided between several custodians, or are they in a single repository?
- Are the records complete, or have some or all been destroyed?

- Did the act establishing the commission specify what should happen to the records when the commission had completed its work?
- Does the national archives law govern the commission records?
- Do any national laws on access to government information pertain to these records?
- At the time the commission closed, was there a national archives, to what part of the government did it report, and what capacities did it have?
- Have the records been used since the commission closed and, if so, for what purposes?

I also wrote to the Washington, D.C., embassy of the countries, told them the purpose of the study, and asked for—and sometimes was granted—an appointment. I interviewed, either in person or by e-mail, former commissioners, commission staffers, commission consultants, human rights activists, and archivists. With the help of the Wilson Center library, I searched periodicals and Web sites. The pertinent sources for each country are listed in the notes.

A few general sources were indispensable. The three-volume *Transitional Justice: How Emerging Democracies Reckon with Former Regimes,* edited by Neil J. Kritz (United States Institute of Peace Press, 1995) and the section on truth commissions on the USIP website (http://www.usip.org) are fundamental sources. The standard book on commissions is Priscilla B. Hayner's *Unspeakable Truths: Facing the Challenge of Truth Commissions* (Routledge, 2002), and the Web site of the International Center for Transitional Justice, where Hayner directs the outreach and analysis unit, is very useful (http://www.ictj.org). For archival laws, the best source remains the volumes of *Archivum,* the review of the International Council on Archives published from 1951 to 2000.

ARGENTINA

At the end of 1983, newly elected president Raul Alfonsin created a National Commission on Disappeared Persons (*Comisión Nacional sobre la Desaparición de Personas,* CONADEP). Its mandate was to "clarify the acts related to the disappearance of persons" and, if possible, determine the location of their remains.

In undertaking its mandate, the commission prepared 7,380 files on the persons who had disappeared and presented 1,086 dossiers to the courts. The files contained "depositions from relatives of the disappeared, testimonies of people released from secret detention centres, and statements by members of the security forces who had taken part in the acts of repression." The commission collected information from "the Armed Forces, the Security Forces and other private and public organizations." Working with the Argentine Centre for Electronic Data Processing (CUPED), the commission selected a data processing method to maintain a list of the victims of repression. CONADEP also produced a television documentary; its officials gave more than thirty press conferences and over one hundred press, radio, and television interviews; and at the end of its existence it "decided to photocopy or microfilm all the documents gathered to date and keep them in safes in official banks." Its final report, the famous *Nunca Mas* (Never Again), was released in September 1984, barely ten months after the commission was created.[1]

Today, the records of CONADEP are held by the Secretary of Human Rights of the Nation (*Secretaría de Derechos Humanos de la Nación*) under the Ministry of Justice, Security and Human Rights of the Nation (*Ministerio de Justicia, Seguridad y Derechos Humanos de la Nación*). This *Secretaría* was established in 1984, just as the commission was terminated, and by executive order the custody of the files was assigned to it. According to *Secretaría* staff, the files are still "used constantly" for the current business of government. In addition, victims, their families, NGOs (both national and international), academics, historians, journalists, students, and investigators have all consulted the records.

The 130 linear meters of records include paper, microfilms, photographs, videotapes, databases, and maps. How much of that quantity is original material from CONADEP and how much has been added during subsequent investigations are unknown, but some quantity is later material. The *Secretaría* has digitized the papers and photographs in the investigatory files and created a relational database to permit easy retrieval. The administrative records of the commission have not had such extensive work, according to the *Secretaría*. No records have been destroyed, and a microfilm copy of certain records has been stored separately in a safety deposit box.[2]

Argentina has a national archives and a national archives law, but at least one of the informed human rights advocates believes that Argentina's archives law is not an adequate "legal norm that regulates the functioning of national archives. Much less this kind of archives."[3] The *Secretaría* reports that the national archives law does not cover the archives of CONADEP.[4]

On February 9, 2004, Argentine president Nestor Kirchner announced that a former navy base would be turned into a museum to commemorate those persons killed during the 1976–1983 dictatorship.[5] He also decreed that a National Archives for Memory (*Archivo Nacional por la Memoria*) would be created under the direction of the *Secretaría*, which could house the archives of CONADEP, among others.[6]

Argentina does not have a freedom of information act or a privacy act.

Contact information:

Directora del archivo
Secretaría de Derechos Humanos de la Nación
Ministerio de Justicia, Seguridad y Derechos Humanos de la Nación
25 de Mayo 606 3er Piso
CP 1002, Ciudad Autónoma de Buenos Aires
ARGENTINA

24321@derhuman.jus.gov.ar
http://www.derhuman.jus.gov.ar

BOLIVIA

The National Commission of Inquiry into Disappearances (*Comisión Nacional de Investigación de Desaparecidos*) was established in 1982 by President Hernan Siles Zuazo to investigate the disappearances of persons under the military dictatorships that ruled Bolivia between 1964 and 1982 and "give accountability." The eight-person panel was headed by the under secretary of the Ministry of the Interior and included representatives of the Human Rights Permanent Assembly (*Asamblea Permanente de Derechos Humanos de Bolivia*) and the association of families (Association of Relatives of the Detained, Disappeared and Martyred for National Liberation). It operated between 1982 and 1984 and did not complete its report before it was disbanded.[7]

The commission originally operated out of the Permanent Assembly's offices, but later moved to its own office space. Some commission documents were produced in triplicate, with one copy retained by the commission and the other two going to the assembly and the family association. Sessions with witnesses were taped. The commission received letters and photographs from the families, as well as reports from investigators and forensic doctors under contract to the commission.[8]

The current location of the records of the commission is unknown; the National Archives of Bolivia (*Archivo General de la Nación*) does not have the records, and the director of the archives is not certain where they are located. She suggests that the Human Rights Permanent Assembly may have the documentation,[9] but this seems unlikely because, according to Priscilla Hayner, the former executive secretary of the commission has "attempted to gain access to the commission's materials in the hopes of publishing a report." [10] If the records were in the custody of the assembly, the former executive secretary would surely have been given access.

Assuming that the records were not destroyed, three possible locations are the archives of the Ministry of the Interior, the presidential archives, or the Library of the Congress. The Ministry of the Interior, among others, has the right to retain its own archives separate from the National Archives. The chair of the commission was in the Ministry of the Interior, so if he retained the records of the commission, they are probably in that archives. Because the president created the commission, the records might have gone to the president's archives. A final possibility is the Library of the Congress, which has tried to obtain records from the last thirty years of the government, justifying its acquisition of recent materials by saying that the National Archives contains more historical material.

The National Archives of Bolivia was established in 1898, and the law governing the archives was last amended in 1989.[11]

Bolivia has no freedom of information act.

BURUNDI

By Resolution 1012 (S/RES/1012) of August 28, 1995, the UN Security Council created an International Commission of Inquiry to "establish the facts relating to the assassination of the President of Burundi on 21 October 1993, the massacres and other related serious acts of violence which followed" and to recommend measures to promote justice and national reconciliation. Secretary-General Boutros Boutros-Ghali appointed to the commission a chairman from Madagascar and four commissioners, all jurists from outside Burundi. The commission had an office in Bujumbura and completed its work in New York. It reported to Secretary-General Boutros-Ghali in July 1996, and he transmitted the report to the Security Council.[12]

In Annex I of the final report, the commission explained its rules of procedure, including the procedures it followed when making tape recordings of testimony, receiving documents from the public, and handling photographs "or other exhibits." Forms used for minutes of hearings and for taking testimony of a witness under oath are appended. The commissioners reported that they heard 667 witnesses in Burundi, Côte d'Ivoire, France, and Uganda. By the time the commissioners left Burundi on May 31, 1996, only "about a third" of the testimonies had been transcribed, and at the time the report was submitted the testimony of about 150 witnesses was still untranscribed.[13] In short, the commission clearly accumulated a substantial body of paper records, audio recordings, and some quantity of photographs and other documents submitted by witnesses, as well as its own administrative records.

In paragraph 64 of the final report, the commissioners wrote, "The body of evidence obtained by the Commission, consisting of documents and recordings, was given into the custody of the Secretary-General of the United Nations." According to the archivist of the United Nations, the records of the commission were in the possession of the UN Department of Political Affairs until the spring of 2004, when fifteen boxes, including five boxes of paper and ten boxes of tapes and transcripts and amounting to about 3 linear meters of records, were transferred to the United Nations Archives.[14]

Contact information:

United Nations Archives and Records Management Section
FF 107
United Nations
New York, NY 10017

http://www.un.org (Go to Welcome / Site Index (bottom of page) / Archives. The researcher application form is in the "Research the archives" section.)

CHAD

In December 1990, the Council of State of Chad, acting on the proposal of the commissioner of justice, issued a decree creating a Commission of Inquiry into the Crimes and Misappropriations Committed by Ex-President Hissene Habre, His Accomplices and/or Accessories. One of the ten stated missions of the commission was "to collect documentation, archives and exploit them."[15]

The commission issued its report in May 1992. In it, the commission declared that "the testimony of 1,726 attestants was recorded by the Commission," although it is not clear whether the testimonies were collected solely on paper (the commission developed "pre-established questionnaires" for four different types of witnesses) or whether some or all were also recorded on audiotape. The report mentions that the commission obtained photographs and ordered exhumations, which means that reports of the exhumations would also be part of the records.[16] In short, the records of the commission were voluminous and varied in physical type.

According to Chad's embassy in Washington, the report and all the records of the commission went to the Ministry of Justice.[17] Efforts to confirm this disposition have not been successful.

The embassy believes that the commission was not a truth commission, but rather an investigating commission on "the former dictator." Because the question of bringing the former president to trial is still current, the embassy thinks "it is still possible" that the findings in the report will be used. Such a possibility means, in effect, that the report and its background information are still active records.

Chad has a national archives, but the law governing the national archives has not been published in the standard professional sources. Consequently, it is not possible to determine whether the records of the Ministry of Justice are to be deposited in the national archives. Chad does not have a freedom of information act or a privacy act.

CHILE

In 1990 the National Truth and Reconciliation Commission was created in Chile by executive order of the new civilian president, Patricio Aylwin Azocar. Known as the "Rettig Commission," after its chair Raul Rettig Guissen, a former senator, the commission was intended to help "clarify in a comprehensive manner the truth about the most serious human rights violations committed in recent years in our country (and elsewhere if they were related to the Chilean government or to national political life), in order to help bring about the reconciliation of all Chileans, without, however, affecting any legal proceedings to which those events might give rise."

The commission obtained copies of documents (including photographs) from government and nongovernment sources, used a database to track cases, and created and maintained case files, general background files, and administrative files. Its investigators took testimony and "recorded" the testimony of the "most important witnesses" (whether this means audiotape or videotape is not known). The commission issued its report to the president in February 1991.[18]

The National Committee of Reparation and Reconciliation, a temporary state body under the supervision of the Ministry of the Interior, succeeded the Rettig Commission in 1992.[19] Writing in 1992, Jorge Correa S., who served as secretary and chief of staff of the commission, reported, "The collected records and data have been kept secret to this day. The Commission [Committee] for Reconciliation, an institution recently established by law, will dispose of them."[20]

With the "expiration of the legal existence" of the committee in 1999, the government established, by executive decree, the Human Rights Program of the Ministry of the Interior. This program was entrusted with four specific tasks, including "[t]o keep and leave in safe custody the documents and files of the former National Committee of Reparation and Reconciliation and those that may be generated by the Program."[21] Logically, then, the program in the Ministry of the Interior would now maintain the documentation that the Rettig Commission passed to the Committee of Reparation and Reconciliation. The records in the Ministry of the Interior are closed other than for official use. In addition, pursuant to Law No. 19,687 of July 4, 2000, the name and particulars of whoever submits useful information to the government for locating missing detainees is secret.[22]

Meanwhile, in 1994, under the guidance of former president Patricio Aylwin Azocar, a nongovernmental organization was established called the Corporation Justice and Democracy. This NGO holds the archives of President Aylwin, including his records related to the Truth and Reconciliation Commission. These presidential materials include a copy of the case files on victims. They may or may not include the materials on the general historical background that the commission collected, and they almost surely do not include the administrative records of the operation of the commission.

In 1995 Chile began the process of nominating the Human Rights Archives of Chile for inclusion in the UNESCO "Memory of the World" project. That nomination included the Truth and Reconciliation Commission records held in the president's files. According to the Memory of the World application, "Once the Commission's mandate concluded, the documentation it had gathered and analyzed was transferred to other agencies, many of which have added or eliminated information. For this reason, the Archive [in the Aylwin records in the Corporation Justice and Democracy] is the only genuine copy that exists of the documentation compiled and analyzed by the Commission." The commission studied 3,877 cases of human rights violations. The files on these cases were copied onto thirty-five optical disks, and copies of the disks were given to the national archives of Chile.[23] The records on the disks are open "only to lawyers and the Courts" as long as trials related to the events documented in the records are continuing.[24]

Chile has an archives law, modified in 1993, and a national archives within the Ministry of Education. It does not have a freedom of information act or a privacy act.

Contact information:

Archivo Nacional de Chile
Correo Central
Miraflores 50
Santiago de Chile
FAX: 562 360 5258

Corporacion Justicia y Democracia:
http://www.focuseurolatino.cl
http://www.justiciaydemocracia.cl

EL SALVADOR

The 1991 UN-moderated peace accord ending the civil war in El Salvador mandated the creation of a Commission on the Truth (*Comisión de la Verdad para El Salvador*). The commission was composed of three persons appointed by the UN Secretary-General after consultation with the Parties to the accord. The commissioners then selected the chair from among the three of them. The commission was given "the task of investigating serious acts of violence that have occurred since 1980 and whose impact on society urgently demands that the public should know the truth," and it was authorized to "[c]arry out any . . . measures or inquiries which it considers useful to the performance of its mandate, including requesting reports, records, documents from the Parties or any other information from State authorities and departments." [25]

The commission staff was located in El Salvador until January 1993, when it relocated to the United Nations in New York City.[26] The commission issued its report on April 1, 1993.[27]

In its report the commission specifically recognized the importance of its archives. Part I of the Introduction described the documentation the commission accumulated, and concluded that "all of this material constitutes an invaluable resource—a part of El Salvador's heritage because (despite the painful reality it records) a part of the country's contemporary history—for historians and analysts of this most distressing period and for those who wish to study this painful reality in order to reinforce the effort to spread the message 'never again.'" The commission then asked:

> What is to be done with this wealth of material in order to make it available to those around the world who are seeking peace, to bring these personal experiences to the attention of those who defend human rights? What is to be done

> when one is bound by the requirement of confidentiality for documents and testimony? What use is to be made of this example of the creativity of the United Nations at a time in contemporary history which is fraught with conflict and turmoil and for which the parallels and the answers found in the Salvadorian conflict may be of some relevance?

The answer the commission proposed was to establish a "Foundation for the Truth" as a not-for-profit academic body in the United States, managed "by an international Board of Directors, with Salvadorian participation; a representative of the Secretary-General of the United Nations and the members of the Commission." The foundation was to be affiliated with the George Washington University International Rule of Law Center in Washington, D.C., where Thomas Buergenthal, one of the three commissioners, was a professor. The commission also recommended that "for those documents which were not subject to secrecy, duplicate copies and computer terminals for accessing the collection would be available in Salvadorian institutions requesting them." The Parties had agreed to this disposition of the records, the commission said, and it proposed inaugurating the foundation in June 1993.[28]

The foundation, however, was never created, apparently because the Jesuits (the Society of Jesus, a Catholic religious order) in El Salvador wanted the records and thus opposed their deposit elsewhere.[29] Thus after completion of the report, the records of the commission were transferred to the United Nations in New York, where they are in the custody of the Secretary-General, but under the control of the UN Archives and Records Management Section. The records include administrative records and general correspondence, case files, documents submitted to the commission, photographs, maps, videotapes and (probably) audiotapes, and diskettes of the database created by the commission. The records are closed to research use.[30]

Despite this unusually explicit background on the proposed disposition of the commission's records, the current legal situation is not at all clear. One could argue that the United Nations is holding the records as a trustee for the Parties, with the understanding that at some time in the future the records will be sent to the government of El Salvador. The commission hinted at this position when it wrote that it held itself "personally responsible for guaranteeing confidentiality before finally handing the archives over to their lawful owners."[31] Alternatively, one could argue that the United Nations, which established and housed the commission, has title to the records and, after considering the effects that release would have on the persons and governments named in the records, can make them available for research use. At present, there is no procedure for making any of the records available to anyone or any program to preserve the records themselves.

At a minimum, the United Nations should acknowledge its trust responsibility for the records and take steps to preserve them. Databases, audiotapes and videotapes, photographs, and even papers need attention if the information they contain is to survive. Storage is not enough: preservation is also required. And, simultaneously with or sequentially to the preservation of the records, the United Nations, with the Parties, needs to clarify the future status of the records. Somewhere, at some time, this "invaluable resource" needs to be available for use.

GERMANY

In May 1992, the German parliament (*Deutscher Bundestag*) established the Commission of Inquiry on Working through the History and the Consequences of the SED Dictatorship (*Enquête-Kommission Aufarbeitung von Geschichte und folgen der SED-Diktatur in Deutschland*). The mandate of the commission was to make contributions both to "political-historical analysis and to political-moral assessment" of the period of SED (Socialist Unity Party of Germany) rule. Two "practical results" to be sought by the commission were "obtaining, securing and opening the pertinent archives" and "improving the conditions for scholarly research on the SBZ/GDR [Soviet Occupation Zone/German Democratic Republic] past."[32] The commission issued its report in June 1994.

The first commission was followed by a second commission, the Commission of Inquiry on Overcoming the Consequences of the SED Dictatorship in the Process of German Unity (*Uberwindung der Folgen der SED-Diktatur im Prozess der deutschen Einheit*), which published its report in 1999. Thereafter, the records of both commissions were transferred to the archives of the German parliament (*Bundestagsarchiv*) in Berlin.

Following on a recommendation of the second commission, parliament established in 1998 a foundation (*Stiftung zur Aufarbeitung der SED-Diktatur*) "to initiate discussion about the second German dictatorship"[33] and to hold most of the records of the commissions. In January 2004, the parliamentary archives transferred the majority of the records of the commissions to the foundation as a loan ("deposit"). The records transferred are about 30 meters in volume and are organized in 302 "Aktenordner [file units]." The records, which are all on paper, consist mostly of the records of hearings and public meetings. The parliamentary archives retains the records of the "administrative work" of the commissions.[34]

The German Federal Archives Law opens records to public use when they are thirty years old. The Federal Archives Law applies to the records of the parliament, except that it does not require parliament to transfer the parliamentary records to the federal archives unless parliament wishes to do so.[35] Because the commissions were parliamentary ones, the thirty-year closure period of the Federal Archives Law applies.

The records held by the foundation that are less than thirty years old can be used if the parliamentary archives agrees: "The Bundestagsarchiv can decide to allow persons to have access to the records before thirty years, especially if there is academic interest." In other words, the foundation holds the records but does not make the access decisions. When the records are thirty years old, they will all be open to "qualified" researchers.[36]

Germany does not have a freedom of information act, but the provisions of the European Union access policy cover it. Germany does have a data protection act.

Contact information:

Stiftung zur Aufarbeitung der SED-Diktatur
Otto-Braun-Str. 70–72
D-10178 Berlin
Germany

Buero@stiftung-aufarbeitung.de
http://www.stiftung-aufarbeitung.de

Deutscher Bundestag
Parlamentsarchiv
Platz der Republik 1
D-11011 Berlin
Germany

http://www.bundestag.de/bic/archiv/index.html

GUATEMALA

A result of the Oslo Agreement of 1994 and the comprehensive peace settlement of 1996 that ended the civil war in Guatemala was establishment of the Commission for Historical Clarification (*Comisión para el Esclarecimiento Historico,* CEH).[37] In February 1997, UN Secretary-General Kofi Annan appointed Christian Tomuschat, a German lawyer, chair ("moderator") of the commission. Tomuschat, in turn, selected two Guatemalan members. The mandate of the commission was to "clarify, with full objectiveness, equity, and impartiality, human rights violations and incidents of violence related to the armed confrontation that have caused suffering to the Guatemalan population" and to prepare, report, and make recommendations to "encourage national harmony and peace in Guatemala."[38]

The UN Office for Projects Services (UNOPS) managed the administrative and budgetary affairs of the commission, although the United Nations "took the view that the CEH, based on an agreement between the Government of Guatemala and the guerrilla organization, was not a UN institution."[39] Because the commission was not a UN institution, the Convention on the Privileges and Immunities of the United Nations did not apply, leaving the archives held by the commission vulnerable to interference by Guatemalan authorities. In response to this situation, in December 1997 the United Nations exchanged formal notes with the government of Guatemala, giving the "documents, records and materials" of the commission the protection of the Convention on the Privileges and Immunities of the United Nations.[40]

After a period of organization, the commission began investigative work in the countryside in September 1997. It conducted 7,200 interviews with some 11,000 persons, and it used a database to provide access paths to the interviews.[41] It obtained copies of declassified items from the U.S. government.[42]

The commission's report was issued in February 1999. Recommendation 49 states:

> That a bill of law be presented by the Government to the Congress of the Republic which quickly and effectively establishes the right of *habeas data* as a specific mechanism of protection and activates the constitutional right, recognized in Article 31 of the Constitution, of access to information contained in archives, files or any other form of state or private record. It should also penalize the gathering, storage or concealment of information about individuals, their religious or political affiliation, their trade union or social activism and any other data relating to their private lives.[43]

The report also recommended that a Foundation for Peace and Harmony be established, whose purpose, among others would be the "promotion of and support for historical research."[44]

On June 8, 1999, UN Secretary-General Kofi Annan issued Bulletin ST/SGB/1999/6, establishing "a special regime for the management, utilization, preservation and disposition of the documents, records and other materials of the Commission for Historical Clarification" in the archives of the United Nations in New York. All transferred materials are sealed, except any records "specifically designated in writing by the Coordinator of the Commission as being for the public domain"—but no such designation appears to have been made. Written authorization of the Secretary-General "signed by the Secretary-General in person" is required to open a sealed container prior to 1 January 2050 "or until such date thereafter as the Secretary-General may specify." The decision to open the records to use requires the Secretary-General to consider the stipulation in the 1994 agreement that "[t]he Commission's proceedings shall be confidential so as to guarantee the secrecy of the sources and the safety of witnesses and informants."

As of late 2003, the records were in New York in the custody of Secretary-General Annan and in the control of the UN Archives and Records Management Section.[45] According to commission chair Christian Tomuschat, "All the pieces of our archives that needed confidentiality were shipped to New York."[46] A memo from the UN's Department of Political Affairs to the UN Archives reports that only the most sensitive records were transferred to the archives and the administrative correspondence was kept in UNOPS, because it was the agency in charge of the management support for the mission.[47] It is not clear whether the UNOPS materials are in New York or remained in Guatemala. All records transferred to the archives are sealed, and no use—including no preservation activity—has been made of them.

At a minimum, the United Nations needs to live up to the promise in the Secretary-General's bulletin to establish a "special regime" for preservation of the commission's records. Databases and papers need attention if the information they hold is to survive. Storage is not enough: preservation is also required.

In addition, the United Nations, with the Parties, should revisit the access conditions of the records. Not all records require protection for fifty years, which the Bulletin ST/SGB/1999/6 recognized by providing that the coordinator of the commission would designate items to be opened. The UN Archives needs to be able to review the records and make a recommendation to the Secretary-General on records that can be made available now (taking over the role of the coordinator), records that may be made available when twenty years old (the standard practice in the UN Secretariat), and records that must be reviewed on January 1, 2050.

By taking on the responsibility for preservation of and access to the commission records, the United Nations is providing an important and entirely appropriate service for the people of Guatemala. Now the United Nations needs to manage the records in accordance with the best professional practices. Fidelity to the promise in the Secretary-General's bulletin will not only preserve and protect the records, but also provide a model for administering commission records that national governments can emulate.

HAITI

In December 1994, President Jean-Bertrand Aristide issued an executive order creating the National Commission for Truth and Justice (*Commission National de Verité et de Justice*). Its mandate was to investigate human rights abuses from the September 30, 1991, coup that overthrew President Aristide until his restoration to power in September 1994. The commission, made up of four Haitian and three international commissioners, presented its report in February 1996.[48]

The commission conducted approximately 6,000 interviews, at least some of which were audiotaped; sponsored forensic examinations of mass graves (the reports of the forensic team included photographs);[49] and produced "a dozen area reports, each of which was hundreds of pages long, combining statistics, secondary materials, analysis of interviews, and direct investigations."[50] The commission also obtained copies of morgue records from the University Hospital in Port-au-Prince and information from NGOs, the United Nations, and the Organization of American States.[51] It is reasonable to assume that some maps also are among the records. The commission used a database to analyze its findings. In short, the records of the commission were voluminous and included most physical types of records.

By 1998 the records of the commission were stored in a special room at the Ministry of Justice, according to a lawyer who had access to them.[52] It is believed that the documents have not been made available to the public, but certain attorneys have been permitted to read and copy documents related to specific cases. The Ministry of Justice has not responded to inquiries about the current location of or access to the records of the commission.

Haiti has a national archives. The national archivist of Haiti stated in October 2003 that he believed the records were divided between the Ministry of Justice and the Ministry of the Interior.[53] The records of both ministries are destined for the national archives.

Haiti has neither a freedom of information act nor a privacy act.

NEPAL

Prime Minister Krishna Prasad Bhattarai established a truth commission in 1990, but it was quickly dissolved and a second commission appointed. The second commission, called the Commission on Inquiry to Find the Disappeared Persons during the Panchayat Period, had a mandate to examine allegations of human rights violations during the 1962–1990 period in which political parties were banned. The commission completed a two-volume report in 1991 that was eventually released to the public in 1994.[54]

In theory, the cabinet secretariat should get the records of the commission.[55] Inquiries to both the secretary of the cabinet and the national archives have not been answered.

Nepal has a national archives.

Nepal has neither a freedom of information act nor a privacy act.

NIGERIA

President Olusegun Obasanjo created the Commission of Inquiry for the Investigation of Human Rights Violations in June 1999. The commission's mandate was to investigate abuses of human rights "and in particular all known or suspected cases of mysterious deaths and assassinations or attempted assassinations" between 1994 and 1999, but that period was later extended back to December 31, 1983. Chaired by former Supreme Court Justice Chukwuditu Oputa and often referred to as the Oputa Panel, the commission originally had a ninety-day mandate, but it was repeatedly extended.

During its investigations, the commission held public hearings, heard evidence from over 2,000 witnesses and collected 1,750 exhibits.[56] The press reported that each witness was required to produce "10 copies of each case submitted." As one onlooker observed, "The peasant economy of Ogoni will collapse if we do so much photocopying."[57] It appears, then, that the records of the commission are voluminous.

The commission completed its work in June 2002 and submitted its eight-volume report to the president, but the report has not been made public.[58]

Nigeria has a national archives, and it adopted a new archives law in 1992. The definition of archives in the law is very broad and specifically covers the records of commissions.[59] Inquiries to the national archives of Nigeria on the location of and access to the records of the commission have not been answered.

Nigeria has a freedom of information act. It does not have a privacy act.

PANAMA

President Mireya Moscoso established Panama's Truth Commission (*Comisión de la Verdad*) by Presidential Executive Decree 2 on January 18, 2001. The commission was asked to investigate and report, as completely as possible, on the murders and disappearances and human rights violations during the military regime, from 1968 until 1989.

According to references in its final report, the commission used a database, audiotaped some meetings, obtained reports from technical specialists and declassified documents from the U.S. government, and received information and photographs from individuals and nongovernmental organizations in Panama. The commission delivered its report in April 2002.[60]

In its report, the commission recommended the creation of a permanent government agency to take over the work of the commission and maintain its files.[61] For a year and a half after the release of the report, an unofficial follow-up committee continued to function, and then on October 20, 2003, by Executive Decree 559, the Truth Commission was extended to December 31, 2004 and renamed the Office for Followup of the Institutional Truth Commission (*Comisión Institucional de la Verdad–Oficina de Seguimiento*). The reauthorized commission reports both to the president and the Ministry of Justice. In January 2004, a consultative committee to the commission was established that includes both government and civil society representatives.[62]

During the interregnum, several ominous events occurred. First, on June 18, 2003, agents of the attorney general raided the Truth Commission's offices in Balboa and seized "skeletal remains, evidence files and financial records" after a criminal complaint was filed by Edwin Wald, an opponent of the commission. The commission in turn filed criminal charges against Wald.[63] Then, on August 15, 2003, the home of Alberto Almanza, director general of the commission and president of the follow-up committee, was burglarized. The thieves "stole three hard drives from computers at a private office he maintains in his home. The hard drives contained information related to the commission's investigation into human rights abuses that took place during the dictatorship. [Almanza] said the intruders also rifled through paper files and took a notebook computer."[64]

Reportedly, the follow-up committee filed a complaint with the Inter-American Commission on Human Rights about the break-ins and the apparent violation of the right to confidentiality of the witnesses and others in connection with the cases.[65] The Inter-American Commission on Human Rights would not confirm this.[66]

Inquiries to the commission, former director-general of the commission, and national archives about the current location of and access to the records have all gone unanswered.

Panama has a national archives that reports to the National Institute of Culture (*Instituto Naciónal de Cultura*).[67] Its habeas data act was passed in 2002. It does not have a privacy act.

PERU

Peru's Truth and Reconciliation Commission (*Comisión de la Verdad y Reconciliación*) was created in 2001 by presidential decree of Valentin Paniagua Corazao "with the approving vote of the Cabinet" to investigate human rights violations between 1980 and 2000—in particular, murders and kidnappings, forced disappearances, serious tortures and other injuries, and violations of the collective rights of the Andean and native communities. Article 7 of the decree declared that "at the end of its functions, the documents and archives that had been successfully obtained by the Commission will be given to the Ombudsman Office, under inventory and with due reserve and confidentiality."[68] According to the coordinator of the Transitional Committee, the ombudsman's office was chosen to hold the records because "the Ombudsman is empowered with the role of supervision in any matter related to human rights. Due to this specific function, it is not rare to have appointed a public and independent institution the task to administer the documentation produced or compiled by the Truth Commission."[69]

The commission eventually accumulated an estimated 200 cubic meters of materials of all physical types: paper, databases, videotapes, audiotapes, photographs, and a few objects.[70] The commission hoped to send "copies of certain documents and electronic records to the United Nations, through the UNDP [UN Development Programme] office in Lima, as a back up."[71] However, the United Nations declined to take the copies.[72]

Although the law establishing the commission clearly specified where the commission records were to go, two problems arose. First, the law on the commission said that the commission's records were to be turned over to the ombudsman, while the national archives law said that all records of state institutions, of which the commission was one, must be transferred to the national archives. Second, the ombudsman had neither the space nor the staff to manage the records. Some Belgian cooperation funds were used to lease space for six months, but that did not cover staff or equipment or supplies.[73] Nor were there funds either to preserve the records or to process and screen them for use by researchers.

The Ombudsman's Office created a Center of Information for the Collective Memory of Human Rights (*Centro de Información para la Memoria Colectiva y los Derechos Humanos*), including the records of the Truth Commission and other related information. It also established a three-person commission to review records and determine which information can be made public and which must be withheld.[74]

Peru has an archives law dating from 1990; the national archives reports to the Ministry of Justice.[75] It also has a freedom of information act and a privacy act.

Contact information:

Centro de Información para la Memoria Colectiva y los Derechos Humanos

http://www.ombudsman.gob.pe

PHILIPPINES

In March 1986, President Corazon Aquino established a Presidential Committee on Human Rights to investigate human rights violations attributed to the military during the 1972–1986 rule of President Ferdinand Marcos. The committee did not issue a final report before it was abolished on May 5, 1987, and its powers were transferred to the Commission on Human Rights.[76] The executive order on the transfer explicitly transferred all records of the committee to the commission.[77]

The committee records in the possession of the present Commission on Human Rights include the records of the administration of the committee, the records of hearings and public meetings, records submitted to the committee by other government bodies, and evidence submitted by private parties. The physical types represented are paper, still photographs, and physical objects. Some records are in the commission's central office, and other records were "forwarded to CHR regional offices." The records sent to the regions included investigation reports of regional offices. Unfortunately, "some got lost while in transit," and others were "destroyed by termites."[78]

The act that established the committee did not include specific guidelines on records management. The government records management regulations were issued in 1988, after the committee closed.[79] The Commission on Human Rights believes that the existing regulations do not cover the records of the committee. Indeed, no records have been sent to the national archives. The commission believes that the national archives does not preserve all the physical types of records found in the committee's files and that it does not have the capacity to preserve the committee's records.[80]

The records have been used by officials of the Ministry of Justice (the case files) and of other government agencies, by legislative bodies looking at budget issues, by victims, by lawyers for the victims, by persons accused by the committee, by lawyers defending the persons accused, and by the general public. According to the commission, journalists, historians, or other academics have not used the records.[81]

The national archives in the Philippines dates from the Spanish colonial period in the nineteenth century, but its history has been "characterized by transfer from one government department to another resulting in the virtual physical odyssey from one place to another." It is now a part of the National Commission for Culture and the Arts. It had no permanent building of its own until work was begun in 1997 to restore a historic building for its use.[82]

The Philippines has both a freedom of information act and a privacy act.

Contact information:

Commission on Human Rights
SAAC Building, Commonwealth Avenue
U. P. Diliman Complex, Quezon City
Philippines

http://www.codewan.com.ph/hrnow/chr/body.htm

REPUBLIC OF KOREA

The Presidential Truth Commission on Suspicious Deaths was established by the Korean parliament in December 1999, and the Special Act to Find the Truth on Suspicious Deaths was signed into law by the president in January 2000.[83] The mandate of the commission was to investigate deaths upon the request of petitioners, to report its findings and recommendations to the president, and to identify human rights perpetrators for prosecution. The terms of the commissioners expired in October 2002; however, in November they were extended for another year, and then extended again until August 2004.[84] The first report of the commission, covering activities from October 2000 through October 2002, was published in January 2003.[85]

The National Archives and Records Service dispatched a staff member to work with the commission. The commission's first report noted this assistance, saying, "An archivist dispatched from the Government Archives created Records Management Guidelines. All collected records, audiotapes, videotapes and photographs will be transferred to the Government Archives."[86]

The commission and the archives agreed that the commission is a public agency covered by the Public Records Management Act. Under that act, the commission will transfer all its records to the national archives when the commission goes out of existence.[87] This transfer has not yet occurred.

In 1997 Korea adopted an Opening of Public Information Act (freedom of information) that applies to public agencies. Presidential commissions are public agencies under the terms of this act, so the truth commission records are covered by it. The act includes a strict privacy exemption clause, which will provide a significant barrier to public access for the foreseeable future.[88] Korea also has a privacy act that applies to the commission records.

SOUTH AFRICA

Created by the parliament in 1995 as part of political negotiations ending South Africa's apartheid government, the Truth and Reconciliation Commission (TRC) of South Africa is the best known of all truth commissions. Its mandate was to investigate human rights violations during the apartheid era between 1960 and 1994, and its records include a wide variety of physical types, from paper to audiotape and videotape, photographs, and electronic documents and databases.[89] The commission issued an interim report in 1998 and, after settling various legal challenges, a final report in March 2003.[90]

As the commission began to wind down in 1999, it transferred all but thirty-four boxes of its records to the National Archives and Records Service. Those thirty-four boxes were sent to the office of the minister of justice, Dullah Omar. In 2003 they were transferred to the National Archives.[91]

In February 2003, the minister of intelligence appointed a Classification and Declassification Review Committee "to advise the government on how to balance requirements of secrecy and open access." The committee, which had members from both the government and civil society, specifically considered the access provisions that should cover the thirty-four boxes of TRC records that were transferred to the National Archives after the bulk of the records.[92] These records are now being reviewed by a multiagency team to make final access determinations.[93]

South Africa has a national archives law, and the National Archives reports to the Ministry of Culture. The National Archives of South Africa Act of 1996 covers the records of the commission.

South Africa has a Promotion of Access to Information Act (no. 2 of 2000 as amended) that controls access to records of the commission.[94] South Africa also has a privacy act.

Contact information:

National Archives of South Africa
Private Bag X236
Pretoria 0001
South Africa

arg02@dacst4.pwv.gov.za

SRI LANKA

In 1978 Sri Lanka adopted a Special Presidential Commission of Inquiry Law, giving the executive broad powers to appoint investigatory bodies. In December 1994, new president Chandrika Bandaranaike Kumaratunge set up three geographically distinct commissions to investigate the disappearance of persons since 1988 and to make charges against those responsible for the abductions. The commissions issued individual interim reports and a consolidated final report in 1997, recommending that legal actions be taken. The report was made public in 1998; compensation was paid to some families of victims; and over four hundred members of the country's security forces were charged with human rights violations. A follow-up commission, the Presidential Commission on Disappearances, began investigations in June 1998 and issued an interim report in January 1999.[95] Another commission, the Presidential Truth Commission on Ethnic Violence, was appointed in 2001 to investigate incidents during the period 1981–1984.[96]

The increasingly frequent appointment of new commissions of inquiry led to questions about their utility. In May 2002, the government announced that it would repeal the Special Presidential Commission of Inquiry Law.[97]

Despite the apparent repeal of the commission law, the records of commissions do exist. According to an official at the Sri Lankan embassy in Washington, the records of the commissions might be either with the records of the president or with the records of the Ministry of Justice. Normally, the records of a presidential commission go to the Presidential Secretariat, which keeps the presidential records. But by an amendment to the Sri Lankan National Archives Law in 1981, the records of presidents are to be transferred to the national archives at the expiration of the term of office of a president. (A departing president can take personal documents but not the presidential records.) Because the president who appointed the commissions is still in office, it is reasonable to assume that the records of the commissions are still in the Presidential Secretariat. Because some of the persons investigated were charged with rights violations, it is possible that these records were sent to the Ministry of Justice for prosecution; the records of the Ministry of Justice also ultimately go to the national archives.[98] Inquiries to the national archives were not answered.

Sri Lanka does not have a freedom of information law or a privacy law.

UGANDA

Uganda has had two truth commissions. The first was established by President Idi Amin Dada in 1974 to investigate accusations of disappearances at the hands of the military forces during the period 1971–1974. The commission heard 545 witnesses and held public hearings.[99] The assistant commissioner for records and information technology wrote in October 2003 that "apparently no report was produced owing to the repressive nature of the Government at that time. Not very helpful but that is the position."[100] However, Amnesty International has a copy of the report on microfiche in its London offices.[101]

In 1986 President Yoweri Museveni established the Commission of Inquiry into Violations of Human Rights to look at human rights violations by state forces from 1962 to 1986. It held public hearings, some of which were broadcast on state-owned radio and television. Its report was issued in 1994, but was not widely distributed.[102]

According to the assistant commissioner, the records of the commission are not in the custody of the department of records; he suggested that "the Office of the President would still be in custody of the full report." To gain access to the records for research, he wrote, "you will require a formal application to the office of the President and or the Uganda National Council for Science and Technology for clearance to access/use the material in question."[103] A second possible location for the records is the Uganda Human Rights Commission. In December 1988, the government established the Uganda Constitutional Commission to draft a new national constitution. The Commission of Inquiry urged the Constitutional Commission to include a permanent and independent human rights commission in the constitution, which it did. The new constitution was enacted in 1995, and the Uganda Human Rights Commission was established by both the constitution and a further act passed by parliament in 1997.[104] It is entirely possible that the records of the Commission of Inquiry were passed to the Uganda Human Rights Commission for its use.

Given the numbers of people interviewed and the public hearings held by both bodies, a sizable set of records should exist. The records are probably largely on paper, perhaps with some photographs. Audiotapes or videotapes also may exist of the public hearings.

Uganda has a national archives. It passed a freedom of information act in 2003, although its implementation depended on the coming into force of Article 41 of the 1995 constitution.[105] It has no privacy act.

URUGUAY

In August 2000, new president Jorge Batlle established a Peace Commission (*Comisión para la Paz)* with a mandate to clarify the fate of those who "disappeared" between 1973 and 1985.[106] This commission followed two parliamentary investigative commissions, one dedicated to investigating the murder of politicians Zelmar Michelni and Hector Gutierrez Ruiz, both senators, and the second devoted to investigating the fate of the "disappeared." In both parliamentary commissions, the majority and the minority created their own reports, and no final report achieved consensus.[107]

The Peace Commission produced a final report in April 2003, but its mandate has been extended to allow it to work on unresolved cases.[108] According to Uruguayan archives professor Alicia Casas de Barran, the commission has made and received "lots" of documents of all physical types: paper, photographs, sound recordings, and electronic data. The Universidad de la Republica has written to the commission offering to take the documents when the commission closes.[109]

The national archives reports to the Ministry of Culture.[110] According to Casas de Barran, Uruguay does not have a "true" archives law, although agencies are required to send records over thirty years old to the national archives. It is unclear whether the archives regulations would cover the records of the Peace Commission. And there are several other complications. First, the national archives primarily holds paper records. Second, staff members in the national archives have served for many years, including through the dictatorship, and commission records turned over to the national archives could be at risk of "some appraisal" and "disposal."[111]

Uruguay has neither a freedom of information act nor a privacy act.

ZIMBABWE

In August 1983, President Robert Mugabe established a Commission of Inquiry to investigate events occurring in Matabeleland in 1983.[112] The chair of the commission was a prominent private lawyer, Simplicious Chihambakwe. The commission began hearing evidence in January 1984.[113] Several months later, the report was presented to the president.

The Catholic Commission for Justice and Peace (CCJP) collected statements from victims that it submitted to the government commission, brought many witnesses, and gave evidence for one and a half days. In addition, the CCJP believes that the three reports it had previously presented to the prime minister were available to the commission.[114] Other than that small bit of information, the types of records made and received by the commission remains unknown. The report has never been made public. In 1997 CCJP and the Legal Resources Foundation, two prominent nongovernmental organizations, published a book on the disturbances in Matabeleland and the Midlands in which they called on the government to make the report of the Chihambakwe Commission available to the public.[115] This did not happen. Recently, human rights groups appealed to the Supreme Court to order the government to make the proceedings of the commission public, but the Supreme Court declined to grant the order.[116]

Zimbabwean law specifies that the records of the Office of the President and Cabinet, the records of the Ministry of Foreign Affairs, and the records of the Intelligence Service are to be closed for fifty years after the date of creation; all other records are closed for twenty-five years. According to the national archivist, when records are transferred to the archives during the closed period, the archives staff do not open the boxes and check each file. Instead, the archives accepts the description of contents that accompanies the transfer and simply stores the records.[117]

The national archives holds records from the Office of the President and Cabinet for the period when the report was written, but the records are in records center storage and the archivist does not know whether the report and its supporting documentation are included in the transferred records. If the records included the administrative records of the commission, such as vouchers, those would have been destroyed in accordance with general records schedules, reports the national archivist.[118]

Recently, the press reported that an agent from the intelligence service had come to the national archives and stolen the commission report. The archivist told the press that "the National Archives is not aware of any theft from our holdings," without specifying whether the report and the commission records are or ever have been in the custody of the national archives.[119]

The national archives was established in 1935, and the current Archives Act dates from 1985.[120]

Zimbabwe adopted a freedom of information law in 2002. In 1986 Zimbabwe passed a Research Act "in terms of which non-Zimbabweans must show either a Research Permit issued by the Research Council of Zimbabwe, or a Temporary Work Permit, before access may be granted."[121] Zimbabwe does not have a privacy act.

NOTES

1. "Argentina: *Nunca Mas*—Report of the Argentine Commission on the Disappeared, September 1984," in *Transitional Justice: How Emerging Democracies Reckon with Former Regimes,* 3 vols., ed. Neil J. Kritz (Washington, D.C.: United States of Peace Press, 1995), 3:3–47; quotes from pp. 46 and 43; "Country Study: Argentina," in ibid. 2:323–381; Priscilla Hayner, *Unspeakable Truths: Confronting State Terror and Atrocity* (New York: Routledge, 2002), 33–34, 316.
2. Laura Saldivia, lawyer, Ministry of Justice, Secretary of Human Rights, Argentina, e-mail message to author, February 9, 2004.
3. Valeria Barbuto, staff member, Memoria Abierta, e-mail message to author, October 6, 2003.
4. Laura Saldivia, e-mail message to author, February 9, 2004.
5. "Argentina to Turn Its 'Auschwitz' into Rights Museum," New York Times Online News Report, February 10, 2004, http://www.nytimes.com.
6. Laura Saldivia, e-mail message to author, February 9, 2004.
7. Hayner, *Unspeakable Truths,* 52–53; confidential interview by author, September 25, 2003.
8. Priscilla Hayner, confidential interview by author, September 25, 2003.
9. Marcela Inch Calvimonte, e-mail message to author, February 10, 2004. The assembly would, of course, have its own copies of commission documents.
10. Hayner, *Unspeakable Truths.*
11. *Archivum,* Vol. 40, 71–76.
12. Letter from Secretary-General to president of the Security Council, July 25, 1996, and annexed final report, S/1996/682, August 22, 1996.
13. Ibid.
14. Bridget Sisk, archivist of the United Nations, e-mail message to author, February 19, May 21, 2004; Angela Schiwy, e-mail message to author, June 2, 2004.
15. "Chad: Decree Creating the Commission of Inquiry into the Crimes and Misappropriations Committed by Ex-President Hissene Habre, His Accomplices and/or Accessories, Decree No. 014/P.CE/CJ/90 (December 29, 1990)," in Kritz, *Transitional Justice,* 3:48–50; quote from p. 48.
16. "Chad: Report of the Commission of Inquiry into the Crimes and Misappropriations Committed by Ex-President Habre, His Accomplices and Accessories (May 7, 1992)," in Kritz, *Transitional Justice,* 3:51–100; quotes from pp. 55–57.
17. Abdoulaye Beri, first counselor, Embassy of Chad, interview by author, September 25, 2003.
18. "Chile: Decree Establishing the National Commission on Truth and Reconciliation and Report of the National Commission on Truth and Reconciliation (February 9, 1991)," in Kritz, *Transitional Justice,* 3:101–168; quotes from pp. 102 and 111.

19. "Administrative, legal, and other initiatives implemented and measures adopted by our democratic governments, intended to avoid the impunity of perpetrators of gross human rights violations committed in our country during the military regime." From President Ricardo Lagos's proposal to the legislature, I-997/02, August 12, 2003, authentic translation provided by the Embassy of Chile, Washington, D.C., copy in author's possession.
20. Jorge Correa S., "Dealing with Past Human Rights Violations: The Chilean Case after Dictatorship," in Kritz, *Transitional Justice,* 3:484.
21. "Administrative," I-997/02.
22. Ibid.
23. UNESCO application in possession of Gloria Alberti, UNESCO regional officer, Chile; reviewed by author, October 22, 2003.
24. Gloria Alberti, e-mail message to author, December 9, 2003.
25. "El Salvador: Mexico Peace Agreements—Provisions Creating the Commission on Truth (Mexico City, April 27, 1991)," in Kritz, *Transitional Justice,* 3:174–176; quote from p. 176.
26. Thomas Buergenthal, "The United Nations Truth Commission for El Salvador," *Vanderbilt Journal of Transnational Law* 27 (October 1994): 497.
27. "From Madness to Hope: The 12-Year War in El Salvador," Report of the Commission on the Truth for El Salvador, United Nations Publication, S/25500, 1993," excerpt in Kritz, *Transitional Justice,* 3:177–215.
28. Ibid., 182.
29. Monique Hand for Thomas Buergenthal, former commissioner, El Salvador Commission on the Truth, e-mail message to author, January 30, 2004. Some of the most famous cases of violence were the murders of Jesuit priests, the murders of four American churchwomen, and the assassination of Archbishop Oscar Arnulfo Romero.
30. Bridget Sisk, e-mail message to author, February 17, 2004.
31. "From Madness to Hope," 182.
32. "Germany: Law Creating the Commission of Inquiry on 'Working through the History and the Consequences of the SED Dictatorship,'" Act No. 12/2597 (May 14, 1992)," in Kritz, *Transitional Justice,* 3:216–219; quotes from pp. 216 and 218.
33. "Stiftung zur Aufarbeitung der SED-Diktatur" (brochure).
34. Matthias Buchholz, archivist, Stiftung zue Aufarbeitung der SED-Dikatur, e-mail message to author, September 24, 2003.
35. Klaus Oldenhage, senior German archivist, e-mail message to author, February 18, 2004.
36. Matthias Buchholz, e-mail message to author, September 24, 2003.
37. "Guatemala: Agreement on the Establishment of the Commission for the Historical Clarification of Human Rights Violations and Incidents of Violence that Have Caused Suffering to the Guatemalan Population (June 23, 1994)," in Kritz, *Transitional Justice,* 3:220–222.

38. Ibid., 220.
39. Christian Tomuschat, "Clarification Commission in Guatemala," *Human Rights Quarterly* 23, no. 2 (2001): 233–258; quote on p. 248.
40. United Nations Secretary-General's Bulletin ST/SGB/1999/6, June 8, 1999; Christian Tomuschat, "Between National and International Law: Guatemala's Historical Clarification Commission," in *Liber amicorum Gunther Jaenicke—Zum. 85 Beburtstag*, ed. Volkmar Gotz et al. (Berlin: Springer, 1998), 991–1011.
41. Audrey R. Chapman and Patrick Bell, "The Truth of Truth Commissions: Comparative Lessons from Haiti, South Africa, and Guatemala," *Human Rights Quarterly* 23, no. 2 (2001): 1–43.
42. Tomuschat, "Clarification Commission," 251: "The CEH enjoyed the active support of the United States, which made available to it numerous documents from different departments, including the Department of State, the CIA [Central Intelligence Agency], the Pentagon, and others." This support is in sharp contrast to the experience of the El Salvador commission; see Buergenthal, "United Nations Truth Commission for El Salvador," section on relations with the United States and the use of the private National Security Archive in Washington, D.C.
43. Commission for Historical Clarification Report, English translation of summary and recommendations, http://hrdata.aaas.org/ceh.
44. Ibid., recommendation 84.
45. Bridget Sisk, e-mail message to author, February 17, 2004.
46. Christian Tomuschat, e-mail message to author, February 4, 2004.
47. Bridget Sisk, e-mail message to author, February 17, 2004.
48. Fanny Benedetti, "Haiti's Truth and Justice Commission," *Human Rights Brief* 3, no. 3 (1996).
49. Brian Concannon, attorney, Bureau of International Lawyers, e-mail message to author, February 5, 2004.
50. Chapman and Bell, "Truth of Truth Commissions," 1–43; quote from p. 24.
51. Benedetti, "Haiti's Truth and Justice Commission."
52. Brian Concannon, e-mail message to author, September 24, 2003.
53. Jean-Wilfrid Bertrand, national archivist of Haiti, interview by author, October 22, 2003.
54. Hayner, *Unspeakable Truths*, 57.
55. Confidential interview by author, September 25, 2003.
56. United States Institute for Peace, "Nigeria," http://www.usip.org/library/truth.html#nigeria (accessed June 27, 2004).
57. Christina Lamb, "Truth Panel Will Call Nigeria's Strongmen to Account," *Electronic Telegraph*, August 22, 1999, http://www.telegraph.co.uk/html (accessed February 13, 2004).
58. UN Office for the Coordination of Humanitarian Affairs, "Nigeria: Rights Panel Submits Report, Calls for Compensation," May 22, 2002, http://www.IRINNews.org.

59. *Archivum,* Vol. 41, 51–61; definitions in article 52.
60. "Informe Final" (*Violaciones a Derechos Humanos de 1968 a 1989*), http://www.defensoriadelpueblo.gob.pa/ (accessed February 12, 2004).
61. *NotiCen,* May 2, 1999; reprinted in "NewsNotes: Panama: Truth Commission Issues Final Report," July/August 2002, 9.
62. Maruquel Patricia Icaza, legal attaché, Embassy of Panama, telephone interview by author, February 18, 2004; Margarita Lacabe, Derechos Humanos, e-mail message to author, February 26, 2004.
63. *Panama News,* June 22–July 19, 2003, http://wwww.ThePanama News.com (accessed February 17, 2004).
64. Ibid., August 17–September 6, 2003.
65. Lisa Mangarrell, attorney, International Center for Transitional Justice, e-mail message to author, February 12, 2004.
66. Ariel Dulitzky, senior specialist, Inter-American Commission on Human Rights, e-mail message to author, February 17, 2004.
67. *Archivum,* Vol. 41, 68.
68. Supreme Decree No. 065–2001–PCM, The President of the Republic, June 4, 2001; confirmed by Supreme Decree No. 101–201–PCM of September 4, 2001.
69. Javier Ciurlizza, e-mail message to author, October 7, 2003.
70. Eduardo Gonzalez, interview by author, November 19, 2003.
71. Javier Ciurlizza, e-mail message to author, October 7, 2003.
72. Eduardo Gonzalez, interview by author, October 7, 2003.
73. Ibid.
74. Eduardo Gonzalez, e-mail message to author, May 17, 2004, forwarding the ombudsman's resolution creating the center.
75. *Archivum,* Vol. 41, 83–87.
76. United States Institute of Peace, http://www.usip.org/library/truth.html#phillipines (accessed February 18, 2004).
77. "All properties, records, equipment, buildings, facilities and other assets of the Presidential Committee on Human Rights shall be transferred to the Commission on Human Rights," Executive Order No. 163, Section 4, May 5, 2004, http://www.codewan.com.ph/hrnow/policy.htm (accessed February 18, 2004).
78. Jacqueline B. Veloria-Meija, director, Commission on Human Rights, Philippines, e-mail message to author, December 2, 2003.
79. *Archivum,* Vol. 41, 88–93.
80. Jacqueline B. Veloria-Meija, e-mail message to author, December 2, 2003.
81. Ibid.
82. http://www.ncca.gov.ph/culture&arts/cularts/heritage/archives/archives-national.htm (accessed September 29, 2003).
83. See the official Web site of the commission, http://www.truthfinder.go.kr/eng/m4.htm (accessed November 12, 2003).

84. "Amnesty International Annual Report 2003, Korea," http://web.amnesty.org/report2003/kor-summary-eng (accessed February 19, 2004); Sangmin Lee, chief consultant archivist, National Archives and Records Service, Republic of Korea, e-mail message to author, September 28, 2003.
85. Translation of parts of the "Report of the Presidential Commission on Suspicious Death; the First Report, 2000.10 to 2002.10" provided by Sangmin Lee, December 9, 2003.
86. Ibid.
87. "Elements of Archival Legislation & the Public Records Management Act (PRMA)," summary translation provided by Sangmin Lee, October 9, 2003; Sangmin Lee, e-mail message to author, September 28, 2003.
88. Sangmin Lee, e-mail message to author, December 9, 2003.
89. Peterson, "Report."
90. "Chronology of South Africa's Truth Commission," Reuters, March 21, 2003, http://www.alertnet.org/thenews/newsdesk/L2174628 (accessed March 22, 2003).
91. "Battle for Access to TRC Files Will Be Heard in Court," *ThisDay* (South Africa), October 30, 2003, 3; Graham Dominy, "A Delicate Balancing Act at the National Archives," *ThisDay* (South Africa), November 17, 2003.
92. Dominy, "Delicate Balancing Act."
93. Graham Dominy, national archivist of South Africa, e-mail message to author, December 8, 2003.
94. Ibid.
95. "Human Rights Watch World Report 1999," http://www.hrw.org/wr2k/Asia-08.htm# (accessed February 19, 2004); United States Institute for Peace, http://www.usip.oprg/library/truth.html#sri_lanka; Amnesty International Index, ASA 37/023/1997, September 4, 1997; K. T. Rajasingham, "Sri Lanka: The Untold Story," *Asia Times,* August 3, 2002, http://www.atimes.com/atimes/South_Asia/DH03Df02.html (accessed February 19, 2004); Hayner, *Unspeakable Truths,* 64–66.
96. Government announcement on official Government of Sri Lanka Web site, August 18, 2001, http://www.priu.gov.lk/news_update/Current_Affairs/ca200108/20010818Truth_commission.htm; *Daily News* (editorial), August 11, 2001, http://www.priu.gov.lk/news_update/EditorialReviews/erev200108/20010811editorialreview.html.
97. *Daily Mirror* (editorial), May 9, 2002, http://www.priu.gov.lk/news_update/EditorialReviews/erev200205/20020509editorialreview.html.
98. Janaka B. Nakkawita, deputy chief of mission of Sri Lanka, Washington, D.C., interview by author, October 3, 2003; National Archives Law No. 48 of 1973, amended in 1981, http://Lawnet.lk (accessed February 19, 2004); "History and Development" (of the National Archives), http://www.mca.gov.lk/D_archives/dept_archives_History.htm (accessed February 19, 2004).

99. Hayner, *Unspeakable Truths,* 51–52; Richard Carver, "Called to Account: How African Governments Investigate Human Rights Violations," *African Affairs* 89 (July 1990): 391–415.
100. Robert Okusam, e-mail message to author, October 20, 2003.
101. Hayner, *Unspeakable Truths,* 276 n. 3.
102. Ibid., 56–57.
103. Robert Okusam, e-mail message to author, November 18, 2003.
104. Human Rights Watch, "Protectors or Pretenders? Government Human Rights Commissions in Africa: Uganda," http://www.hrw.org/reports/2001/africa/uganda/uganda.html (accessed February 19, 2004); Carver, "Called to Account."
105. Uganda, Freedom of Information Center, http://foi.missouri.edu/internationalfoi/index.html.
106. U.S. Department of State, Bureau of Democracy, Human Rights, and Labor, *Uruguay, Country Reports on Human Rights Practices, 2002,* March 31, 2003, http://www.state.gov/g/drl/rls/hrrpt/2002/18347.htm; "Amnesty International Annual Report 2001," http://web.amnesty.org/web/ar2001.nsf/webamrcountries/URUGUAY?OpenDocument (both accessed February 20, 2004).
107. Hayner, *Unspeakable Truths.* 53–54; Aldo Marchesi, e-mail message to author, October 19, 2003.
108. "Comunicado de Prensa sobre informe final de Comision para la Paz," April 28, 2003, http://www.uruguay.indymedia.org/news/2003/04/13072.php (accessed February 20, 2004).
109. Alicia Casas de Barran, e-mail message to author, January 13, 2004; interview by author, October 21, 2003.
110. *Archivum,* Vol. 41, 257–258.
111. Alicia Casas de Barran, e-mail message to author, January 13, 2004.
112. Hayner, *Unspeakable Truths.,* 51; Carver, "Called to Account," 391–415.
113. Michael Auret, former chair, Catholic Commission for Justice and Peace, Zimbabwe, e-mail message to author, February 9, 2004.
114. "Breaking the Silence, Building True Peace: A Report on the Disturbances in Matabeleland and the Midlands 1980–1989. Summary Report," Part One, Data Sources, http://www.hrforumzim.com/members_reports/matrep/matrepintro.htm; Michael Auret, e-mail message to author, February 9, 2004.
115. "Breaking the Silence," Part Four, Recommendation 1.
116. David Coltart, e-mail message to author, February 7, 2004.
117. Ivan Munhamo Murambiwa, national archivist of Zimbabwe, interview by author, October 23, 2003.
118. Ibid.
119. Ibid.
120. *Archivum,* Vol. 41, 268–272.
121. Ibid., 269.

APPENDIX A

Criteria for Distinguishing Commission Records from Personal Property

Official records of the commission should be maintained separately from the personal papers of commissioners or staff members. Individuals should decide at the time of original filing whether an item should be designated a record or a personal paper. If this decision has not been made before the close of the commission, all materials in each staff member's office should be retained and sent to the subsequent custodian of the records, who will have to determine which materials are personal papers and thus can be returned to the staff member and which must be retained as records of the commission itself.

Some commissioners and staff members may wish to retain duplicates of items that are in the official files. In these cases, the commission or the subsequent custodian must decide whether the duplicate can be given to the individual. If the item is public, such as a copy of a press release, it may be safely retained. If, however, the duplicate is of the minutes of a meeting held in executive session or an item related to a case investigated by the commission that contains information not yet made public, then it is inappropriate to allow such documents to be in private hands until the official copy is opened.

In determining which items are personal and which items are official, it is useful to ask a series of questions. The following questions are a sample of those that are relevant:

1. *Creation.* Was the document created by a commissioner or staff member of the commission on commission time, with commission materials, at commission expense? (If not, then it very likely is not a "commission record" on that basis alone.)
2. *Content.* Does the document contain "substantive" information? (If not, then it very likely is not a "commission record" on that basis alone.) Does it contain personal as well as official business information?

3. *Purpose.* Was the document created solely for an individual employee's personal convenience? Alternatively, to what extent was it created to facilitate commission business?
4. *Distribution.* Was the document distributed to anyone else for any reason, such as for a business purpose? How wide was the circulation?
5. *Use.* To what extent did the document's author actually use it to conduct commission business? Did others use it?
6. *Maintenance.* Was the document kept in the author's possession, or was it placed in an official commission file?
7. *Disposition.* Was the document's author free to dispose of it at his personal discretion? What was the actual disposal practice?
8. *Control.* Has the commission attempted to exercise "institutional control" over the document through applicable maintenance or disposition regulations? Did it do so by requiring the document to be created in the first place?
9. *Segregation.* Is there any practical way to segregate out any personal information in the document from official business information?
10. *Revision.* Was the document revised or updated after the fact for record-keeping purposes?

APPENDIX B

Access Criteria

In his influential 1996 report to the United Nations Commission on Human Rights on the question of impunity of perpetrators of human rights violations, the distinguished legal scholar Louis Joinet proposed five principles on the "preservation of and access to archives bearing witness to violations." Joinet was exclusively concerned with the government records made and received during the period in which the violations took place. The Joinet principles are as follows:

PRINCIPLE 13. Measures for the Preservation of Archives

The right to know implies that archives should be preserved. Technical measures and penalties shall be applied to prevent any removal, destruction, concealment or falsification of archives, especially for the purpose of ensuring the impunity of perpetrators of human rights violations.

PRINCIPLE 14. Measures for Facilitating Access to Archives

Access to archives shall be facilitated in order to enable victims and persons related to claim their rights.

Access should also be facilitated, as necessary, for persons implicated, who request it for their defence.

When access is requested in the interest of historical research, authorization formalities shall normally be intended only to monitor access and may not be used for purposes of censorship.

PRINCIPLE 15. Cooperation Between Archives Departments and the Courts and Extrajudicial Commissions of Inquiry

The courts and extrajudicial commissions of inquiry, as well as the investigators reporting to them, must have free access to archives. Considerations of national security may not be invoked to prevent access. By virtue of their sovereign power of discretion, however, the courts and extrajudicial commissions of inquiry may decide, in exceptional circumstances, not to make certain information public if such publication might jeopardize the preservation or restoration of the rule of law.

PRINCIPLE 16. Specific Measures Relating to Archives Containing Names

(a) For the purposes of this principle, archives containing names are to be understood to be those archives containing information that make it possible, in any way whatsoever, directly or indirectly, to identify the individuals to whom they relate, regardless of whether such archives are on paper or in computer files.
(b) All persons shall be entitled to know whether their name appears in the archives and, if it does, by virtue of their right of access, to challenge the validity of the information concerning them by exercising a right of reply. The document containing their own version shall be attached to the document challenged.
(c) Except where it relates to top officials and established staff of those services, information relating to individuals which appears in intelligence service archives shall not by itself constitute incriminating evidence, unless it is corroborated by several other reliable sources.

PRINCIPLE 17. Specific Measures Related to the Restoration of or Transition to Democracy And/or Peace

(a) Measures shall be taken to place each archive centre under the responsibility of a specifically designated person. If that person was already in charge of the archive centre, he or she must be explicitly reappointed by special decision, subject to the modalities and guarantees provided in principle 41;
(b) Priority shall initially be given to inventorying stored archives and to ascertaining the reliability of existing inventories. Special attention shall be given to archives relating to places of detention, in particular when the existence of such places was not officially recognized;
(c) The inventory shall be extended to relevant archives held by third countries, who shall be expected to cooperate with a view to communicating or restituting archives for the purpose of establishing the truth.[1]

The Joinet principles also could be applied to the records of a truth commission that seeks to reveal the human rights violations it has uncovered. The following discussion, in the spirit of the principles, focuses specifically on the issues of access to commission records.

The purpose of an access policy for the records of a truth commission is to define the balance between the public's right to know about activity by the commission and the rights of individuals to protect information about themselves from premature or harmful public disclosure. In addition, it must acknowledge the legitimate protectible interests of government.

It is easy to say that files on victims should be restricted from public access, except with the consent of the victim, and that the records of the commission, acting as an official body, should be open. Yet an examination of the complexity of the records suggests that this formulation, while right in its essentials, has to be more carefully stated in order to avoid some foreseeable harm.

Two propositions should guide decisions: (1) that all records of the commission will, at some time in the future, be open for public inspection and research use; and (2) that all records already made public or records of public events should remain open. The length of time that records must be closed varies, depending on the nature of the records and the national ethos on privacy and the state of security in the country.

The records of a commission fall into three categories: investigative records, program records, and administrative records. Each is considered separately in the rest of this appendix.

INVESTIGATIVE RECORDS

In most commissions, the investigative records are case files on victims (actual or asserted) of human rights violations. Commissions may also have investigative files that focus on particular incidents or geographic areas, as well as investigative case files on alleged perpetrators. Some commissions may have case files of persons seeking amnesty for real or alleged human rights abuses. Each type must be considered separately for purposes of access by the public.

Records on Victims of Human Rights Violations

Two principles form the basis for handling the records of victims of human rights violations:

1. The victim has the right to know what information is in the file on his or her case (habeas data).
2. The victim has the right to determine whether the file on his or her case can be consulted by third parties.

In all cases, "victims" should be understood to include "heirs and assigns." Often the file is on a person who is deceased, and the privacy interest in it is now that of the living heirs. This situation is especially significant when the files contain genetic information obtained from heirs during the forensic investigation of remains.

The victim can see the file. In the postcommission period, the victim or the victim's family must have the right to understand exactly what the commission did and learned about the case. Two questions about access by the victim or the family to the case file immediately arise: What about the security classified documents that may be associated with a case? What about the names of third parties?

Classified documents are a serious issue. Some classified documents are key pieces of evidence, but unless steps are taken to declassify them, the victim would not be permitted to see these important items. The commission must either request the creating agency to declassify all documents in possession of the commission *or* use a legal process available to the state as a whole, such as a presidential order or parliamentary proclamation, to declare that all classified documents used in the course of the work of the commission are declassified. Once the documents are declassified, then any other considerations, such as privacy for third parties, can still be asserted.

Third parties mentioned in the records are also a complex issue. First, the records may reveal that persons who were in the service of repressive state bodies committed acts leading to the victim's fate. Second, the records may mention persons who were in the service of repressive state bodies in connection with an incident or allege that they committed an act, but the connection or allegation may not be proven. Third, other people not in the service of the repressive bodies may have given information to the commission. Fourth, persons not in the service of the repressive bodies may be mentioned in the statements given by others or in documents obtained by the commission.

The question here is the potential for violent revenge. Both individual rights and the health of a fragile new democracy must be considered. The refusal to disclose the names of those responsible for crimes or injuries to the victims is incompatible with democracy. But so is action by the government, such as opening files, that would broadcast allegations by or about persons who have had no prior warning and therefore no chance to defend themselves.

Three possible courses of action are to close the documents mentioning third parties, to redact[2] the names of the third parties, or to provide notice to the third parties that documents mentioning them are about to be released. Providing notice (for example, through publication of notice in the government gazette or through individual mailings for which individual addresses must be found) is the most laborious, but it also provides the victim with the most information and provides the persons named with safeguards. Once notice is given and a suitable waiting period has elapsed to give the third party the opportunity to review the document naming him and to take any legal remedies, then the victim should be permitted to see the entire file on the case.

The victim controls access. The victims of repression, or their heirs, should control access to the files on their cases for a fixed period. If the existence of a case file on the victim has not been made public by the commission, the victim's right to control access extends to the fact of the existence of the file. In these cases, the archives simply refuses to confirm or deny whether a case file exists.

During the closed period, the victim should be permitted to request that the case files be opened. Some victims of state security agencies in Central European countries have wanted the files opened, but the existing laws permit only access by the victim and do not allow the victim to instruct the state to open the files. The victim should be able to provide authorization for specific persons, such as an attorney or a health worker, to see the files or to authorize them to be opened to the public.

Public officials in pursuance of official business are allowed access. If the case of the victim is still open at the time the commission closes and the case is referred to the public prosecutor or other official, then those persons have access to the case file. In the future, however, the public prosecutor may investigate a case possibly linked to a case investigated by the commission and that is closed to public use. Although it may be in the interest of the government to have access to the commission's file, the victim's rights of control also must be respected. The public prosecutor and other government officials (excluding the staff maintaining the commission's archives in their custodial duties) should have access to the file only if a court or other judicial authority determines that the file is essential for the prosecution of the case and the victim is notified and has the right to object. In this instance, the prosecutor may have a copy of the file only for the duration of the investigation, and the copy must be returned to the archives. In no circumstances should the original file be withdrawn from the archives and given to another public body.

The victim may have a copy. Some victims, particularly those who have no or minimal literacy, may find it easier to have a copy of the files that they can read outside a government reading room. This puts access totally in the hands of the victim and may lead to an anomalous situation: the archives has not been authorized by the victim to release the file to the public, but the victim is making the information available. On balance, however, the importance to the victim of having a copy outweighs the possible incongruity.

Because of the sensitivity of the information, the victim should receive the copy of the case files in person, or should authorize a designated agent to receive it. The copy should not be sent through the mail or through a commercial delivery service, unless the victim specifically requests it.

The victim and those named may submit further information. Both victims and those named in the files may want to make corrections or declarations about the information in the files. The original case files, as they existed at the close of the commission, should not be altered by additions or deletions. The archival custodian should accept the submissions, create a new file in which the submissions are placed, and place a cross-reference in the original file indicating that a parallel file exists. This cross-reference must be incorporated in both the paper and electronic files. The archives will ensure that the parallel file is always given to researchers who request the original file.

The files of persons the commission determined were not victims should be handled in a manner similar to that used for the files of victims. For various reasons, some persons are not accorded the status of victims—a decision that is not a reflection of either their integrity or the process the commission used to make determinations. The information in any case files on persons not accorded the status of victims is as important to them as the information in victim files is to those persons who were officially recognized as victims and should be handled by the same careful process.

Records of Incident and Geographic Investigations

Of all the investigative files, the records of incident and geographic investigations are the easiest to open. The most important issue in reviewing these records for disclosure is to ensure that any information that might identify the person who provided it under a promise of immunity is protected. This information includes not only names and personal identifiers (e.g., social services numbers), but also descriptions that would lead the informed reader directly to the individual (e.g., "the woman who did the laundry for the priest" or "the family who lived next to the church"). Redaction, as discussed earlier in the context of third parties named in victim case files, is one alternative.

Records on Alleged Perpetrators

Information contained in files on alleged perpetrators may be relevant to historical events; information *may* relate to criminal activities. As it is for victims' case files, if the case is still open at the time the commission closes and the case is referred to the public prosecutor or other official, then those officials will have access to the case file. In the event of a prosecution, the normal rules of access by the accused and the attorneys for the accused would apply.

The more difficult case is when a file exists on an alleged perpetrator but no further official action is undertaken. One of the principles of handling the case files on victims—that the victim has the right to know what information is in the file on his or her case (habeas data)—is important here. As Joinet says in Principle 14, "Access should also be facilitated, as necessary, for persons implicated, who request it for their defence." The second general principle—that the victim has the right to determine whether the file on his or her case can be consulted by third parties—is more troublesome when applied to alleged perpetrators. The files on these persons are often of keen interest to the general public. Does the right to control access to the contents of the files extend to perpetrators as it does for the victims? One possible approach is to require all persons seeking access to a file on an alleged perpetrator to apply through a court or other judicial body. That body would determine, on a case-by-case basis, whether the archives would be permitted to confirm or deny that a file exists and, with court approval and after redaction, to make it available for review.

Records of Amnesty Applicants

Applicants with public hearings. The records of amnesty applicants have a special status, because public disclosure of the deeds committed is part of the amnesty process. It follows, then, that the fact that a file exists on the applicant is public, as are the essential parts of the case. Although the case file may contain some incidental information not presented in public, the public knowledge of the case is so extensive that the case files should be public, whether the amnesty has been granted or not.

The principal problem in amnesty case files is that third parties are mentioned in the files, both persons who were victims and persons who are alleged to have been perpetrators. If the amnesty case was heard in a public hearing and these names were revealed, they can also be released in the case file. If, however, the case file contains additional names, release cannot be made until further steps are undertaken. One option is to require judicial review like that needed for access to the case files of alleged perpetrators. A second option is a notification process, whereby archives officials would read the file, identify the persons named therein, and inform them of the intent to open the file. Notification could be made through publication in the government gazette or through individual letters (for which addresses must be found). If the gazette option is possible, it would be the less laborious route, but it would disclose publicly that something about the person appears in a file of the commission. After notification, the person notified must have the right to see the portion of the file pertaining to him or her, but the archives first must redact the documents to eliminate the parts that do not relate to the party who will review.

Applicants who had no public hearing. The reasons for rejection of an amnesty application vary. In character, these files most resemble those of the alleged perpetrators whose cases were not prosecuted, and therefore the same considerations would apply.

PROGRAM RECORDS OF THE COMMISSION

In the interest of demonstrating the essential fairness of the commission process, most program records of the commission should be made available for public research use at the time of transfer to archival custody. The principal concern should be to protect the names and identities of victims, third parties, and others to whom confidentiality was promised. If such information is found in the minutes of meetings, for example, the minutes must be redacted prior to release.

ADMINISTRATIVE RECORDS OF THE COMMISSION

In general, the administrative records of the commission can be opened to public access after transfer to archival custody. Two exceptions are personnel records of the commission staff and witness protection records.

Personnel Records

Some commission staff members may be on loan from other government agencies; some may be on contract. All have files, whether paper or electronic, providing details of their employment with the commission. Files may also exist for applicants who were not selected for positions with the commission. Each of these individuals has some expectation of confidentiality about the information contained in these files, and each will need to document his or her employment with the commission for future employers or for pension purposes. It is important that the records be retained and be accessible for such uses.

Often the staff members of a commission are not employees of the government's civil service. Although it might be possible to deposit the records of the commission's employees with the government's central personnel office, that could mean mixing the records of these non–civil service status employees with those of civil servants. It probably makes more sense to keep the records of non–civil service status employees with the records of the commission, but to require the archival custodian to handle them, in access terms, just like the central government handles the records of its civil servants.

The records of those not selected for commission posts should be transferred to the archival custodian, should not be accessible, and should be reviewed for possible destruction.

Witness Protection Records

Records on the protection of witnesses are another special category. The truth commission in South Africa had a formal arrangement for the protection of witnesses. Witness protection files are highly sensitive technical files that explain the steps taken to protect the person. Because of the need to protect the witness over his or her lifetime, the records must remain with a government body able to give this service. When a commission with a witness protection program closes, it needs to notify all protected witnesses that it intends to transfer its witness protection program records to the government agency operating the witness portection program. The protected witness should be given an opportunity to raise any objections to the transfer of his or her file. If a witness objects, the file should be transferred to the archives and closed, except to the witness. The files should be opened only upon the death of the witness or, if the date of death is unknown, fifty years from the initiation of witness protection. Files in the custody of the operating office should be transferred to the archives at the time of the death of the witness or in fifty years, whichever comes first.

NOTES

1. "The Administration of Justice and the Human Rights of Detainees: Question of the impunity of perpetrators of human rights violations (civil and political).

Revised final report prepared by Mr. Joinet pursuant to Sub-Commission decision 1996/119," United Nations Commission on Human Rights, Sub-Commission on Prevention of Discrimination and Protection of Minorities, E/CN.4/Sub.2/1997/20/Rev.1, October 2, 1997. For an archival view of access to records of security services, see Antonio Gonzalez Quintana, "Archives of the Security Services of Former Repressive Regimes: Report prepared for UNESCO," UNESCO, Paris, 1997.

2. "Redact" means to take out. The most common method used by archivists is to make an electrostatic copy of the original document, either cut out or blacken the information to be withheld, and make a copy of the document with the holes or blackened areas. The latter copy is the one released to the user. In instances in which the document to be redacted is electronic, or if it is scanned, it can be redacted electronically, but the archives must ensure that the space where information was withheld is clearly marked on the new copy, such as with ellipses or the words "Information withheld."

APPENDIX C

Physical Storage Criteria

The following tables showing physical storage criteria were excerpted from the Draft International Standard ISO/DIS 11799 of 1998, "Information and documentation—Documents storage requirements for archive and library materials."

Table C.1 Climatic Data

	Temperature min. (°C)	Temperature max. (°C)	Temperature variation	RH[a] min %	RH max %	RH variation
Paper optimum	2	18	±1	30	50	±5
Paper in use	14	18	±1	30	50	±5
B&W[b] photo film, polyester base		Less than 21	±2	30	50	Avoid cycling
Color photo film, polyester base		Less than 2	±2	25	30	Avoid cycling
B&W photo prints	2	20	4/day	30	50	Avoid cycling
Color photo prints		Less than 2		30	50	Avoid cycling
B&W microfilm, polyester base		Less than 21	±2	30	40	Avoid cycling
Magnetic media (data, audiotape, videotape)	17	20		20	30	Avoid cycling

a. Relative humidity.

b. Black and white.

Table C.2 Maximum Limits for Air Pollutants

	Parts/billion (by volume)
Sulphur dioxide (SO_2)	5–10
Nitrogen oxides (NO_x)	5–10
Ozone (O_3)	5–10

Index

Printed in the United States
67770LVS00003B/81-88

9 780801 881725